INDIAN COINS

GRUNDRISSS
DER
INDO-ARISCHEN PHILOLOGIE
UND
ALTERTUMSKUNDE

UNTER MITWIRKUNG VON.

GEORG BUHLER

FORTGESETZT

F. KIELHORN.

INDIAN COINS

BY

E. J. RAPSON

WITH FIVE PLATES

GYAN

Published by

GYAN

Gyan Publishing House
5, Ansari Road
Daryaganj, New Delhi-110002
Phone: 011-47034999, 9811692060
E-mail: books@gyanbooks.com

Distribution Network
gyanbooks.com
India, USA, Canada, UK, Australia, France

ISBN : 978-81-212-2560-1 (HB)
First Published, 1898

2nd Impression 2021

Printed at: Gyan Press, Delhi.

Indian Coins
Author: E. J. Rapson

II. BAND, 3. HEFT, B.

Subskriptionspreis M. 5.—.
Einzelpreis „ 6.—.

GRUNDRISS

DER

INDO-ARISCHEN PHILOLOGIE

UND

ALTERTUMSKUNDE

UNTER MITWIRKUNG VON

A. BAINES-LONDON, R. G. BHANDARKAR-PUNA, M. BLOOMFIELD-BALTIMORE, J. BURGESS-EDINBURGH, J. F. FLEET-LONDON, O. FRANKE-KÖNIGSBERG, R. GARBE-TÜBINGEN, W. GEIGER-ERLANGEN, K. GELDNER-BERLIN, G. A. GRIERSON-CALCUTTA, A. HILLEBRANDT-BRESLAU, H. JACOBI-BONN, J. JOLLY-WÜRZBURG, H. KERN-LEIDEN, E. KUHN-MÜNCHEN, E. LEUMANN-STRASSBURG, B. LIEBICH-BRESLAU, H. LÜDERS-GÖTTINGEN, A. A. MACDONELL-OXFORD, R. MERINGER-WIEN, R. PISCHEL-HALLE, E. J. RAPSON-LONDON, J. S. SPEYER-GRONINGEN, M. A. STEIN-CALCUTTA, G. THIBAUT-ALLAHABAD, A. VENIS-BENARES, SIR R. WEST-LONDON, M. WINTERNITZ-PRAG, TH. ZACHARIAE-HALLE

BEGRÜNDET

VON

GEORG BÜHLER

FORTGESETZT

VON

F. KIELHORN.

INDIAN COINS

BY

E. J. RAPSON

WITH FIVE PLATES.

—

STRASSBURG
VERLAG VON KARL J. TRÜBNER
1898.

VERLAG VON KARL J. TRÜBNER

In diesem Werk soll zum ersten Mal der Versuch gemacht werden, einen Gesamtüberblick über die einzelnen Gebiete der indoarischen Philologie und Altertumskunde in knapper und systematischer Darstellung zu geben. Die Mehrzahl der Gegenstände wird damit überhaupt zum ersten Mal eine zusammenhängende abgerundete Behandlung erfahren; deshalb darf von dem Werk reicher Gewinn für die Wissenschaft selbst erhofft werden, trotzdem es in erster Linie für Lernende bestimmt ist.

Etwa dreissig Gelehrte aus Deutschland, Österreich, England, Holland, Indien und Amerika haben sich vereinigt, um diese Aufgabe zu lösen, wobei ein Teil der Mitarbeiter ihre Beiträge deutsch, die übrigen sie englisch abfassen werden.

Besteht schon in der räumlichen Entfernung vieler Mitarbeiter eine grössere Schwierigkeit als bei anderen ähnlichen Unternehmungen, so schien es auch geboten, die Unzuträglichkeit der meisten Sammelwerke, welche durch den unberechenbaren Ablieferungstermin der einzelnen Beiträge entsteht, dadurch zu vermeiden, dass die einzelnen Abschnitte gleich nach ihrer Ablieferung einzeln gedruckt und ausgegeben werden.

Der Subskriptionspreis des ganzen Werkes beträgt durchschnittlich 65 Pf. pro Druckbogen von 16 Seiten, der Preis der einzelnen Hefte durchschnittlich 80 Pf. pro Druckbogen. Auch für die Tafeln und Karten wird den Subskribenten eine Ermässigung von 20% auf den Einzelpreis zugesichert. Über die Einteilung des Werkes giebt der auf Seite 3 dieses Umschlags befindliche Plan Auskunft.

STRASSBURG, im Oktober 1901.

Die Verlagshandlung.

The Encyclopedia of Indo-Aryan Research contains the first attempt at a complete, systematic and concise survey of the vast field of Indian languages, religion, history, antiquities, and art, most of which subjects have never before been treated in a connected form. Though the Encyclopedia is primarily intended as a book of reference for students, it will nevertheless be useful to all connected with India and though it chiefly summarises the results achieved, it will also contain much that is new and leads up to further research.

About thirty scholars of various nationalities, — from Austria, England, Germany, India, the Netherlands and the United States — have promised to unite order to accomplish this task. The contributions will be written either in English or in German.

Each part will be published separately and with a separate pagination.

The subscription for the complete work will be at the rate of about 65 Pfennig (8 d), the price of a single part at the rate of 80 Pfennig (10 d), per sheet of 16 pages. Subscribers will also enjoy a reduction of 20 percent for plates and maps.

For the plan of the work see page 3 of this cover.

The Publisher.

☞ Bei Begründung des Grundrisses war in Aussicht genommen, die einzelnen Hefte später in drei Bände zusammenzufassen und jedem dieser Bände ein Gesamtregister für die darin enthaltenen Hefte beizugeben. Da aber die bis jetzt erschienenen Hefte einen weit grösseren Umfang einnehmen als ursprünglich dafür angesetzt war und das Bedürfnis für Register zu den einzelnen Heften sich als dringend herausgestellt hat, haben sich Herausgeber und Verleger entschlossen, besondere Register für jedes Heft herzustellen.

Dem hier vorliegenden Heft sind Indices beigefügt; für die bereits erschienenen Hefte liegen fertig vor die Indices zu:

- I. 3b: Zachariae, Die indischen Wörterbücher.
- I. 6: Speyer, Vedische und Sanskrit Syntax.
- I. 8: Pischel, Grammatik der Prakrit-Sprachen.
- I. 10: Geiger, Literatur und Sprache der Singhalesen.
- II. 1b: Bloomfield, The Atharvaveda.
- II. 3b: Rapson, Indian coins.
- II. 8: Jolly, Recht und Sitte.
- III. 1a: Macdonell, Vedic Mythology.
- III. 2: Hillebrandt, Ritual-Literatur.
- III. 4: Garbe, Sāṃkhya und Yoga.
- III. 8: Kern, Manual of Indian Buddhism.

Die Verlagshandlung.

Die Vervielfältigung

ENCYCLOPEDIA OF INDO-ARYAN RESEARCH

EDITED BY G. BÜHLER

VOL. II, PART 3, B.

SOURCES OF INDIAN HISTORY: COINS.

BY

E. J. RAPSON.

I. INTRODUCTION.

§ 1. **Limits of the Contribution.** — The object of this contribution is to give an account from the historical point of view of all the known coinages of ancient and mediaeval India, beginning with the earliest times and extending in each particular instance to a period determined by the following considerations. In the case of the states of Northern India generally, and those also of Southern India which were situated to the north of the river Kistna, our subject is naturally bounded by those well-defined limits which are, as a rule, afforded by the introduction of the Muhammadan form of coinage as a result of the progress of Muhammadan conquest between c. 1000 and 1310 A.D. In the extreme south, where Muhammadan supremacy was never absolute, and where, consequently, no similar break of continuity occurs in the coinage, our survey will not extend beyond the rise of the kingdom of Vijayanagar in 1326 A.D.

Beyond these limits reference will, however, be made to any note-worthy instance in which, from some special cause, such as the isolation or inaccessibility of a state, the use of an early form of coinage has survived until a later date.

§ 2. **Classification.** — Ancient and mediaeval Indian coins, as thus defined, fall naturally into three main classes — (1) a primitive native coinage, which, so far as the present state of our knowledge will allow us to judge, seems to have been very widely used throughout India and in Ceylon; and, following this, the classes which numismatists have usually distinguished geographically as (2) Northern, and (3) Southern. These terms are not strictly accurate, as any rigid geographical classification is, in this case, impossible. The real distinction between the two classes so called is due to the disturbing influence of foreign invasions; and, while it is true that all the successive waves of foreign influence came in at the N. W. corner of India, it is equally true that most of them had spent their force not only before reaching the south, but even before reaching the centre or the north-east. On the other hand, intercourse with the north gave to the coinage of certain southern states, e. g. that of the Andhras, some of the usual northern characteristics. In the numismatic sense, therefore, the term 'Northern' should be understood as denoting that class of Indian coins in which the primitive native system of coinage is very greatly modified by foreign influence, and the term 'Southern' as denoting that class in which, for the most part, an independent and distinctively Indian development is to be traced.

§ 3. **Literature.** — The following are standard works on the different branches of Indian numismatics. Further references are given in or at the end of each section.

(1) *Graeco-Bactrian and Indian generally* — H. H. WILSON, Ariana Antiqua, 1841; J. PRINSEP, Essays on Indian Antiquities (originally published in JBA. 1832—38), edited and supplemented by E. THOMAS, 1858.

(2) *Graeco-Bactrian, Graeco-Indian, and early Indo-Scythic* — A. CUNNINGHAM, Coins of Alexander's Successors in the East, 1873 (= NChr. 1868, pp. 93. 181. 257; 1869, pp. 28. 121. 217. 293; 1870, pp. 65. 205; 1872, p. 157; 1873, p. 187); A. VON SALLET, Nachfolger Alexander d. Gr. in Baktrien und Indien, 1883 (= ZfN. 1879, pp. 165. 271; 1880, p. 296; 1881, pp. 109. 279; 1882, p. 158; 1883, p. 156), For a list of previous works on the subject v. p. 79 (= ZfN. 1879, p. 283), and also PE. II, p. 172, note; P. GARDNER, Catalogue of Indian Coins in the British Museum: Greek and Scythic Kings of Bactria and India, 1886; G. BÜHLER, Kharoṣṭhī Inscriptions on Indo-Grecian Coins, WZKM. VIII, p. 193.

(3) *Indo-Scythic* — E. DROUIN, Chronologie et Numismatique des Rois Indo-Scythes, 1888 (= Rev. Num. pp. 8. 185); A. CUNNINGHAM, Coins of the Indo-Scythians (i. e. Śakas and Kuṣanas), 1892 (= NChr. 1888, p. 199; 1889, p. 268; 1890, p. 103; 1892, pp. 40. 98); id., Coins of the Later Indo-Scythians, (i. e. Later Great Kuṣanas, Scytho-Sassanians, Little Kuṣanas, and Ephthalites or White Huns), 1894 (= NChr. 1893, pp. 93. 166. 184; 1894, p. 243), Résumé by V. A. SMITH, JBA. 1894, p. 179; E. DROUIN, Monnaies des Grands Kouchans (i. e. the Scytho-Sassanians of C.) Rev. Num. 1896, p. 154.

(4) *Native States* — E. THOMAS, Ancient Indian Weights, 1874 (= International Numismata Orientalia I, Part 1); A. CUNNINGHAM, Coins of Ancient India, 1891; id., Coins of Mediaeval India, 1894; BHAGVĀNLĀL INDRAJĪ, Coins of the Western Kṣatrapas (ed. RAPSON), JRAS. 1890, p. 639; V. A. SMITH, Coinage of the Early or Imperial Gupta Dynasty of Northern India, JRAS. 1889, p. 1; id., Observations on the Gupta Coinage, JRAS. 1893, p. 77; id., History and Coinage of the Gupta Period, JBA. 1894, p. 164.

(5) *Southern India* — W. ELLIOT, Coins of Southern India, 1886 (= International Numismata Orientalia III, Part 2).

(6) *Ceylon* — T. W. RHYS DAVIDS, Ancient Coins and Measures of Ceylon, 1877 (= International Numismata Orientalia I, Part 6).

II. EARLIEST NATIVE COINAGE.

§ 4. Standard and date of use. — The most ancient coinage of India, which seems to have been developed independently of any foreign influence, follows the native system of weights as given in Manu VIII, 132 ff. The basis of this system is the *rati* (*raktikā*), or *guñja*-berry, the weight of which is estimated at 1,83 grains = ,118 grammes. Of the gold standard coin, the *suvarṇa* of 80 *ratis* = 146,4 grs. or 9,48 grms., no specimens are known; but of the silver *purāṇa* or *dharaṇa* of 32 *ratis* = 58,56 grs. or 3,79 grms., and of the copper *kārṣāpaṇa* of 80 *ratis* (same weight as the *suvarṇa*), and of various multiples and sub-divisions of these, numerous examples have been discovered in almost every part of India.

The estimate of the weight of the *rati* here given is that of CUNNINGHAM, CAI. p. 44. For other estimates v. TH. AIW. p. 65; SMITH, Proc. BA. 1887, p. 222, and JRAS. 1889, p. 42. For the complete system of native weights, v. C.ASR. X, 78; XIV, 17; and TH.AIW. p. 13. Cp. also AR.V (1798), p. 91; JBA. 1838, p. 892; 1864, p. 251; 1865, pp. 14. 46. 51.

The earliest specimens of this coinage are probably at least as early as the beginning of the 4th cent. B.C.

C.ASR. I, p. 70; II, pp. 229. 264. 288; XIV, p. 17; C.NChr. 1873, p. 209; C.CAI. p. 52; TH.AIW. p. 33; RH.D.ACC. p. 1, summary of results p. 13, § 22; RAPSON, JRAS. 1895, p. 869.

In the N.W. the influence of the Greek settlers in the early part of the 2nd cent. B.C. greatly modified this coinage; but, in other parts of India, this primitive coinage continued for some centuries longer (Th. AIW. p. 57).

§ 5. Form of the coins. — The shape of these coins is approximately square or oblong, the silver coins having been, as a rule, cut from a flat sheet of metal, and the copper coins from a bar. These primitive coins are little more than weights of metal, on which was stamped from time to time the symbol of the authority responsible for their correctness and purity. From this method of marking, they have usually been called *punch-marked* coins (**Plate I, 1**).

C.CAI. p. 42, Pl. I, 1—23; C.ASR. VI, 213; Th.AIW. p. 57; Collection of symbols, Theobald, JBA. 1890, p. 181 (rev. Rev. Num. 1892, p. 91); 1894, p. 73. Cp. also Ar. Ant. p. 403; JBRA. X, p. xxi.

§ 6. Guild-tokens. — To the same period belong the pieces (**Plate I, 2**) which Bühler has recognised as *guild tokens* (Indian Studies III[2], p. 49; cp. C.CAI. p. 63, Pl. III, 8—12); and, perhaps of a slightly later date, the pieces of *cast copper*, which, like these, bear inscriptions in Indian characters of an ancient form or designs of purely native art unmodified by any foreign influence (e. g. C.CAI. Pl. II, 21. 22).

Cp. also C.CAI. p. 59, Pl. I, 24—29; PE. I, p. 214; Th.AIW. p. 55.

III. EARLY FOREIGN COINS IN INDIA.

§ 7. Early Persian Coins. — During the period of Achaemenid rule (c. 500—331, B.C.) *Persian* coins circulated in the Panjab. Gold double *staters* (**Plate I, 5**) were actually struck in India, probably in the latter half of the 4th cent. B.C. (E. Babelon, Les Perses Achéménides, pp. xi. xx. 16, Pl. II, 16—19, and 27). Many of the silver *sigloi*, moreover, bear countermarks so similar to the native punch-marks as to make it seem probable that the two classes of coins were in circulation together (**Plate I, 3**), and this probability is increased by the occurrence on sigloi of characters which have been read as Brāhmī and Kharoṣṭhī letters (**Plate I, 4**).

Bühler, Indian Studies III[2], p. 113; Rapson, JRAS. 1895, p. 865. Babelon, op. cit. p. XI, attributes these countermarks to other provinces of Asia.

§ 8. Early Persian standard. — As a result of the Persian occupation is probably to be regarded the establishment in the Panjab of a weight-system apparently derived from the Persian (siglos = 86,45 grs., or 5,601 grms.), which was subsequently used in the coinages of nearly all the Greek princes.

Gard. p. lxviii; C.NChr. 1888, p. 216, explains this change of standard as due to an alteration in the relative value of gold and silver; von Sallet also, ZfN. 1879, p. 193, regards the new standard as reduced from the Attic.

§ 9. Athenian coins. — At an early period, the *owls* of Athens were carried in the course of commerce to the East; and, when the supply from the Athenian mint grew less (i. e. for about a century before B.C. 322, when the mint was closed) imitations were made in N.India. Some of these are merely attempts to faithfully reproduce the originals (**Plate I, 6**); others, probably somewhat later in date, substitute for the owl on the reverse an eagle (**Plate I, 7**). From the latter class, the coins of Sophytes (v. inf. § 11), who, at the time of Alexander's invasion (326 B.C.) ruled over a district on the banks of the Acesines, seem to be copied. (**Plate I, 8**).

Head, Catalogue of Greek Coins in the Brit. Mus., Attica, pp. xxxi. xxxii, Athens, nos. 267—276a, Pl. VII, 3—10; Gardner, NChr. 1880, p. 191, Pl. X, 5. 6. Cp. also C.NChr. 1866, p. 220; Gard. p. xix.

§ 10. Alexander's coins. — It is probable that certain copper coins of square Indian form, bearing the name ΑΛΕΞΑΝΔΡΟΥ, were struck in India by Alexander the Great.

GARD. p. XVIII. DANNENBERG who first noticed these coins attributed them to Bactria, VON SALLET, ZfN. 1879, p. 285, Pl. IV, 1.

§ 11. Indian relations with the Seleucids. — From the date of the eastern expedition of Seleucus and his alliance with Candragupta in B.C. 306 (Appian, Syr. 55), a constant intercourse was maintained between the Seleucid kingdom of Syria and the Maurya kingdom of N.India, as is shown by the Seleucid embassies established under Megasthenes and Daimachus at the court of Pāṭaliputra, and by the mention of Greek kings in Aśoka's inscriptions (LIA. II, p. 241). The adoption of the elephant as a type on Seleucid coins, and the similarity between certain coins of Seleucus (e. g. BABELON, Rois de Syrie, Pl. I, 15) and those of Sophytes, are no doubt due to this intercourse.

It has been generally assumed (e. g. GARD. p. XX) that the coins of Sophytes were copied from those of Seleucus; but the opposite may have been the case, or, perhaps, both of these classes may have been derived from the same originals — the imitations of Athenian coins made in India (v. s. § 9). For Sophytes, v. C.JBA. 1865, p. 46; NChr. 1866, p. 220; Geog. Ind. p. 157; VON SALLET, ZfN. 1879, p. 285, Pl. IV, 2; GARD. pp. XIX. 2, Pl. I, 3; SYLVAIN LÉVI, JA. 1890 (XV), p. 237. Cp. also NChr. 1893, p. 101; Proc. BA. 1867, p. 106; Rev. Num. 1890, p. 496; ZfN. 1883, p. 2, Pl. I, 1.

§ 12. Graeco-Bactrian influence. — But, until the beginning of the 2nd cent. B.C., no extensive modification of the native Indian coinage had been caused by foreign influence. It was from the kingdom of Bactria, established by Diodotus (**Plate I, 9**), who revolted from the Seleucid sovereign Antiochus II, c. B.C. 248, that there came eventually the influence which completely changed the form and character of the coinage of N.W.India (v. inf. § 18).

§ 13. Parthian influence. — Parthian characteristics, due no doubt to the contact between Parthians and Śakas in Bactria, are found in the Saka coinages of India, the earliest of which — those of Maues — belong to the latter half of the 2nd cent. B.C. (v. inf. § 29). The dynasty of Vonones, which seems to have exercised a sort of suzerainty over the successors of Maues in the 1st cent. B.C., is very probably Parthian in origin (v. inf. § 30). The later dynasty of Gondophares in the 1st cent. A.D. is certainly Parthian (v. inf. § 61).

§ 14. Roman coins, dating from the beginning of the empire onwards are found in great numbers in many parts of India both north and south (v. inf. §§ 69. 123).

AR. II (1790), p. 331; C.ASR. II, p. 162; XIII, p. 72; JBA. I (1832), pp. 392. 476; 1834, pp. 562. 635; 1851, p. 371; Proc. BA. 1879, pp. 77. 122. 205. 210; 1880, p. 118; 1886, p. 86; NChr. 1843 (V), p. 202; 1843 (VI), pp. 111. 160; 1891, p. 199; PE. I, p. 148.

§ 15. Roman influence. — With regard to their influence on Indian coinages, two points at least seem clear — (1) the head on the Kuṣana copper coins bearing the name Kozola Kadaphes is directly imitated from the head of Augustus (v. inf. § 66); (2) the gold coinage of the Kuṣanas follows a weight-standard identical with the Roman (v. inf. § 70).

§ 16. Sassanian influence. — The result of intercourse between the Sassanian monarchy of Persia and the Kuṣana kingdom of Kabul, during the period from c. A.D. 300 to 450, is shown by a class of coins struck in the Oxus territory and known as Scytho-Sassanian — a class which is of great chronological importance from the fact that most of the issues can be attributed to the different Sassanian monarchs who reigned within these limits (v. inf. § 75). There is also further evidence of relations between Persia and India during the reign of VarahrānV, A.D. 420—438 (DROUIN, HE. p.24, from the Muséon 1895). But the most extensive importation of Sassanian coins into India was due to the invasion of the Hūṇas (last quarter of the 5th cent. A.D.), who brought with them the proceeds of the plunder of Sassanian treasuries. Some of the coins thus introduced were restruck in *repoussé* by the Hūṇas (v. inf. § 104); others no doubt were used as currency with little or no modification and formed the patterns from which subsequent Hūṇa and also other Indian coinages were copied (v. inf. § 105). In this manner the Sassanian type of coin — *Obv.* King's Head: *Rev.* Fire-Altar — became firmly established in certain parts of India, and continued to be used during several centuries (v. inf. § 122). During the 7th cent. also, as is proved by the coins, Sassanian kingdoms existed in Multan and Sind (v. inf. § 109).

IV. GRAECO-INDIAN COINS.

§ 17. The Greek invasion. — The incursions of the Bactrian princes into the Kabul Valley and Northern India must have begun about the beginning of the 2nd cent. B.C. The war between the Seleucid Antiochus III and the Bactrian Euthydemus ended in an alliance between them (B.C. 206). Probably in the same year, Antiochus crossed the Paropanisus and renewed friendly relations with the king then reigning in the Kabul Valley, Sophagasenus or Subhagasena, who has been identified (L.IA II, p. 273) with Jaloka.

POLYBIUS, Exc. Hist. XI, 34, 11.

§ 18. Euthydemus and Demetrius. — It was during the reign of *Euthydemus* (Plate I, 18), and, perhaps, under the leadership of his son Demetrius, that the first Indian conquests were made (GARD. p. XXII). As evidence of this early settlement in India, there exists a coin of *Demetrius* which is, perhaps, the first to show the result of a compromise between the Greek and Indian methods of coinage (Plate I, 10). The regular types of the Greek system are retained, but the coin is of the square Indian form, and, on the reverse, is added an Indian translation in Kharoṣṭhī characters of the Greek legend on the obverse.

C.NChr. 1869, p. 136, Pl. IV, 11; GARD. Pl. XXX, 3. For the extent of the Indian conquests of Demetrius, v. VON GUTSCHMID, Gesch. Irans, p. 44, and GARD. p. XXIII.

§ 19. Eucratides. — Next, in point of date, come the Indian conquests of *Eucratides*, c. B.C. 190—160, the rival and conqueror of Demetrius (JUSTIN XLI, 6). His coins are found at Balkh, in Seistan, in the Kabul Valley, and, more rarely, in the Panjab.

C.NChr. 1869, p. 217, Pll. VI. VII. For the date of Eucratides: VON SALLET, ZfN. 1879, p. 170; GARD. p. XXVI. Parthian coins attributed to Mithradates I (B.C. 171—138) imitated from those of Eucratides: GARD., Parthian Coinage, p. 32, Pl. II, 4 (= Internat. Num. Orient. I, Part 5). — Gold piece of 20 staters struck by Eucr.: CHABOUILLET, Rev. Num. 1867, p. 382, Pl. XII, »Les textes relatifs à Eucratide«, id. p. 407. Gold coin of Eucr.: MONTAGU, NChr. 1892, p. 37, Pl. III, 11. Cp. also ZfN. 1879, p. 295. Silver medal (decadrachm) attributed to Eucratides or Heliocles, GARD., NChr. 1887, p. 177, Pl. VII, 1. Coins of Eucratides bearing also the name of Heliocles and Laodice: VON SALLET, ZfN. 1879, p. 188; VON GUTSCHMID, Gesch. Irans, p. 48; GARD. p. XXIV.

§ 20. Dates on G.I. coins. — Important for the chronology of this period is the unique tetradrachm of *Plato*, copied from the tetradrachm of Eucratides, and bearing the date 147 of the Seleucid era = B.C. 165. The occurrence of other dates on Bactrian coins is less certain.

GARD. p. 20, Pl. VI, 11; VAUX, NChr. 1875, p. 1; VON SALLET, ZfN. 1879, pp. 173. 190. Cp. also Proc. BA. 1872, pp. 34. 174; C.NChr. 1869, p. 226; 1892, p. 45; HOERNLE, Ind. Ant. 1879, p. 196; TH.JRAS. 1877, p. 3; VON SALLET, ZfN. 1879, p. 184.

§ 21. Pantaleon, Agathocles. — Contemporary with the reign of Eucratides in India are those of *Pantaleon* and *Agathocles,* whose coins are found both in the Kabul Valley and W.Panjab — those of Agathocles also as far south as Kandahar (C.NChr. 1869, p. 41). The Indian coins of these two rulers are the only coins of Greek princes which bear inscriptions in Brāhmī characters (**Plate I, 12**, Pantaleon). Certain copper coins of Agathocles have legends on both *obv.* and *rev.* in Kharoṣṭhī letters (**Plate I, 16**).

C.NChr. 1868, p. 279, Pl. VIII, 8—10, Pl. X; VON SALLET, ZfN. 1879, 175, Pl. V; GARD. p. XXVI, Pll. III, 8. 9, IV, and XXX, 4. For the reading of the Kharoṣṭhī legends on coins of Agathocles: BÜHLER, WZKM. VIII, p. 206.

§ 22. Agathocles. — Certain *medals* (tetradrachms) of Bactrian fabric struck by Agathocles bear the portraits, types, and inscriptions of Alexander the Great, Antiochus 'Nicator' (*sic*, v. VON GUTSCH., Gesch. Ir., p. 38; GARD. p. XXVIII, note), Diodotus, and Euthydemus; similar medals of the Bactrian prince Antimachus also bear those of Diodotus and Euthydemus.

GARD. Pl. IV, 1—3, and XXX, 5. 6. (The medal of Antimachus and Euthydemus is in the possession of an Indian coin-dealer, and is as yet unpublished). For the historical significance of these: VON SALLET, ZfN. 1879, p. 176; 1881, p. 279; GARD. p. XXVIII. Cp. also NChr. 1868, p. 278; 1869, p. 31; 1880, p. 181; PE. I, p. 28.

§ 23. Antimachus. — The types on the coins of *Antimachus* point to some naval victory won by him, perhaps on the Indus or some other large river.

GARD. pp. XXIX. 12, Pl. V, 1—3; C.NChr. 1869, p. 39.

§ 24. Heliocles. — After the reign of *Heliocles* (c. B.C. 160—120) the transference of the Greek power from Bactria to territory south of the Paropanisus was complete. Until his time, many of the Greek princes had ruled both in Bactria and in India, and had struck coins both of Bactrian fabric bearing purely Greek legends, and of Indian fabric with bilingual inscriptions. Up to this date all the silver coins were struck according to the Attic standard (drachm = 67,5 grains or 4,37 grammes). This Attic standard gradually gives place to the Persian standard (v. sup. § 8). Heliocles himself, Apollodotus I, and Antialcidas use both standards; all the later Greek princes use the Persian standard only.

VON SALLET, ZfN. 1879, p. 193; GARD. p. LXVII.

§ 25. Heliocles' successors. — The reigns of all the Greek princes who ruled after the date of Heliocles — they are about 20 in number according to the coins — must be confined within about a century, i. e. from c. 120 B.C. to 20 B.C., when the Kuṣanas completed the conquest of India. There were undoubtedly, for a considerable portion of this period, two or more distinct dynasties of Greek princes ruling at the same time, and varying greatly from time to time in power and extent of territory. No perfectly satisfactory arrangement of these different families or of the chronology of this period has yet been proposed.

For one suggested arrangement: C.NChr. 1868, p. 274. Available data and general chronological table: GARD. p. XXXII ff. »Die sicheren Daten«: VON SALLET, ZfN. 1879, p. 191. Historical notices of Menander and Apollodotus: GARD. p. XXXVI; L.IA. II, p. 322; PE. I, p. 47; RH.D., SBE. XXXV, p. XIX; VON GUTSCHMID, Gesch. Ir., p. 104. Coin bearing the names of Archebius and Philoxenus (the genuineness of this specimen and of others struck from the same dies has been disputed): VON SALLET, ZfN. 1888, p. 9, Pl. I, 3; id. 1896, p. 327. Coin of Polyxenus: RODGERS, NChr. 1896, p. 269; of Theophilus, SMITH, JBA. 1897, p. 1. Interpretation of monograms: C.NChr. 1846, p. 175; 1868, p. 181; 1888, p. 204; CHABOUILLET, Rev. Num. 1867, p. 393; TH. JRAS. 1863, p. 121; PE. I, p. 55; VON SALLET, ZfN. 1879, p. 200; GARD. p. LV; HOERNLE, Ind. Ant. 1879, p. 196. The metal nickel used for Bactrian coinage: FLIGHT, NChr. 1868, p. 306.

V. SCYTHIC INVADERS OF INDIA.

§ 26. The chronological difficulties of the history of Northern India during the last two centuries B.C. are not, however, confined to the Greek dynasties. The coins bear witness to the existence, during this period, of two well-defined dynasties of Scythic origin, of other Scythic powers less clearly marked, and of a number of native Hindu states.

§ 27. The Śaka invasion. — The history of these Scythic tribes which came in contact with the Greek kingdoms in Bactria and India is known from Chinese sources.

For a list of these: DROUIN, Rev. Num. 1888, p. 13.

For a consideration of their numismatic remains, the following main dates and facts will be sufficient.

At the time of the establishment of the Bactrian monarchy, the territories to the north — Sogdiana and Transoxiana — were occupied by a tribe called the Sse (or Sek), who had come from the south of Çhina.

These Sse have usually been identified with the Śakas, who, in previous ages, had come into conflict with the Achaemenid and Macedonian powers. In B.C. 165, the Sse were expelled from Sogdiana by the Yueh-chi, who were themselves flying before the Hiung-nu. The Śakas, thus dispossessed, invaded Bactria. From this period until the fall of the Bactrian monarchy, the Greeks had to contend against both Parthians and Śakas, while the Parthian and Śakas were alternately the friends and foes of one another. It is, perhaps, to this association with the Parthians that the earliest Śaka coins of India owe certain Parthian characteristics (v. inf. § 29). The Yueh-chi, who now held the ancient territories of the Śakas, in turn invaded and gained complete possession of Bactria, c. 120 B.C. This was no doubt the immediate cause of the first Śaka invasions of India. About a century later, or c. 25 B.C., one of the five tribes of the Yueh-chi, the Kuṣaṇas, gained the supremacy over the others, crossed over the Paropanisus, destroyed the last vestiges of Greek rule in the Kabul Valley, and subsequently conquered the whole of Northern India.

SPECHT, JA. 1883, p. 317 (cp. Ind. Ant. 1886, p. 19); DROUIN, Rev. Num. 1891, p. 217 = JA. 1891 (XVII), p. 145. But see S. LÉVI, JA. 1897, p. 1 ff.

§ 28. Śaka imitations of older coins. — To the period of Śaka rule in Bactria belong the barbarous imitations of Macedonian, Seleucid, Bactrian, and Parthian coins. These coins are, in general, mere imitations, and their inscriptions are debased copies of the Greek inscriptions; but on a few specimens there are legends which have been recognised as the most ancient examples of the Aramaean writing of Turkestan (**Plate I, 18. 19,** Euthydemus: a Bactrian original, and a Śaka copy).

C.NChr. 1889, p. 301, Pl. XIII; DROUIN, Rev. Num. 1891, p. 222; 1894, p. 174; id. Rev. Sémitique 1893, p. 173; C.CAI. p. 35; PE. I, p. 30.

§ 29. Maues, Moa. — The earliest of the Śaka dynasties in India is that of *Maues* or *Moa*, who is probably to be identified with the Moga of the Taxila copper-plate grant (BÜHLER, EI. IV, p. 54; BH.JRAS. 1894, p. 551). His date is probably not later than c. 120 B.C. This agrees with the fabric of his coins, which are superior in workmanship to those of the later Greek princes, and with the fact that some of them are directly imitated from the coins of the earlier Greek princes, e. g. Demetrius and Apollodotus (Plate I, 14, imitated from Demetrius, GARD., Pl. III, 2). The form of inscription used by Maues — ΒΑΣΙΛΕΩΣ ΒΑΣΙΛΕΩΝ ΜΕΓΑΛΟΥ — (Plate I, 15) is of Parthian origin (v. sup. § 13), and first occurs on the coins of Mithradates I (c. B.C. 171—138). The coins of the dynasty of Maues are found in the Panjab only — particularly in the N.W. — and *not* in Afghanistan (C.NChr. 1890, p. 104). It has accordingly been conjectured (GARD. p. XLI; DROUIN, Rev. Num. 1888, p. 20; and JA. 1891 (XVII), p. 146 = Rev. Num. 1891, p. 219) that this band of Śakas, unlike other foreign invaders, entered India by the Karakoram Pass, and passed through Kashmir into the Panjab. C., however, denies the possibility of this, and supposes that, after the Śaka occupation of Arachosia and Drangiana — the country afterwards called Śakasthāna — a detachment under the leadership of Maues passed thence into Sind and up the valley of the Indus.

C.NChr. 1890, p. 103; GARD. p. 68, Pl. XVI; VON SALLET, ZfN. 1879, p. 334; 1882, p. 161; 1883, p. 159. Cp. also Ar. Ant. p. 300; JBA. 1840, p. 1008; NChr. 1861, p. 72; PE. II, p. 200.

§ 30. Vonones. — Nearly allied to the dynasty of Maues is that of *Vonones* (Plate I, 17: Vonones and Spalagadama), the coins of which are found in the country around Kandahar and Ghazni, the ancient Arachosia, and in Seistan, the ancient Drangiana. The Parthian appearance of the names of these princes is most striking; and, consequently, the term Indo-Parthian has sometimes been applied to them. In support of their Parthian origin may also be adduced the fact that the same territory was, in the 1st cent. A.D., governed by an undoubtedly Parthian dynasty — that of Gondophares (§ 61) to which, in this article, the designation Indo-Parthian is restricted. At the same time, it is certain that the dynasties of Maues and Vonones were intimately connected, and it is difficult to separate them so far as to call the former Śaka and the latter Parthian. The difficulty is, perhaps, to be explained by supposing the existence among the Śakas of this period of a strong Parthian element due to previous events.

§ 31. Vonones, Azes. — As Vonones strikes coins together with Azes, the successor of Maues, his date is probably c. 100 B.C. What the exact relations between these two ruling families of Śakas or Śaka-Parthians were, it is impossible to say; but it is noticeable that, whenever they strike coins in common, the members of Vonones' family invariably occupy the obverse, and the members of Maues' family the reverse. To judge from other analogous instances in ancient numismatics, this fact would seem to show that the former exercised some sort of lordship over the latter.

It would seem probable, that, while the dynasty of Vonones ruled over Arachosia and Drangiana (Sakasthāna), and the dynasty of Maues over the valley of the Indus (i. e. both W.Panjab and Sind) with its capital at Taxila, the E.Panjab (capital Śākala), and the Kabul valley, were still, for the most part, governed by Greek princes (C.NChr. 1890, p. 109).

C.NChr. 1890, p. 106, Pl. VII.

§ 32. Satraps of Mathurā. — As Śaka satraps must probably also be classed the Satraps of Mathurā (or Northern Kṣatrapas), probably of the second half of the 1st cent. B.C., on whose history so much light has been thrown by the inscriptions on the Mathurā Lion Capital (Bhagvānlāl Indrajī, ed. BÜHLER, JRAS. 1894, p. 525), and other inscriptions from the same neighbourhood (BÜHLER, EI. II, p. 195).

For their coins: C.CAI. p. 85, Pl. VIII; and BH. ed. RAPSON, JRAS. 1894, p. 541. Cp. also JBA. 1854, p. 679; PE. II, p. 223; SMITH, JBA. 1897, p. 9, Pl. I, 15.

§ 33. Rañjubula. — Important chronological data for the period of these satraps of Mathurā are the following: — (1) the first satrap, *Rañjubula* (**Plate II**, 5) who is undoubtedly the Rājula of the Lion Capital, strikes a coinage directly imitated from that of the Greek prince Strato II (**Plate II**, 4), (2) the Great Satrap Kusulaa Patika of the Lion Capital is almost certainly to be identified with the Satrap Patika, son of Liaka Kusuluka, of the somewhat earlier Taxila copper-plate grant, dated in the 78th year of the Great King Moga (v. supr. § 29, BÜHLER, EI. IV, p. 54, and BH.JRAS. 1894, p. 552). Another class of the coins of Rañjubula, on which the name is written Rājubula in Brāhmī characters (**Plate II**, 6), and the coins of the Satraps of Mathurā generally are related as regards both types and fabric to those of Pañcāla (Suṅgas) and those of the Hindu princes of Mathurā (v. inf. §§ 52. 53).

§ 34. Other Śaka Satraps. — The attribution of certain other classes of Scythic coins previous to the period of Kuṣana supremacy is, at present, more doubtful. Some of these are imitated from the coins of the successors of Maues — Azes and Azilises; and, as they bear the title 'satrap', they were very probably struck by satraps of this dynasty. The date of one of these, the Satrap *Zeionises* (Jihonisa, **Plate II**, 3), son of the Satrap Manigula is probably as early as 80 B.C. (C.NChr. 1890, pp. 125. 168, Pl. XV, 1, 4a). Of a similar date is *Aspavarma*, son of Indravarma, the *strategos* of Azes (id. pp. 126. 169; but v. also inf. § 61), and a ruler, whose name has not yet been discovered and who is only known at present as the son of Vijayamitra (id. pp. 127. 170). Somewhat later are the badly executed coins of *Kharamosta*, son of Artas (id.).

For the suggested identification of this *Kharamosta* with the *Kharaosta* of the Mathurā Lion Capital, v. BÜHLER's note JRAS. 1894, p. 533.

§ 35. Doubtful Classes. — The precise nationality of the following Scythic princes, whose coins seem all to belong to the latter half of the 1st cent. B.C., is uncertain.

Miaus or *Heraus* (**Plate II**, 1), the former reading of the name being that which was finally adopted by C. (NChr. 1888, p. 47). Formerly the Śaka nationality of this ruler was accepted, and a portion of the legend on his tetradrachms was read ΣΑΚΑ ΚΟΙΡΑΝΟΥ, 'prince of the Śakas' (GARD. p. XLVII). OLDENBERG read ΣΑΚΑ-ΚΟΡΡΑΝΟΥ, 'the Saka-Kuṣana', regarding the Kuṣanas as a *family* of the Śakas (cp. the title of Kaniṣka, *Guṣanavaṃśa-saṃvarddhaka*), and the Śakas and Yueh-ti as either the same people, or the Śakas as one of the tribes of the Yueh-ti (ZfN. 1881, p. 295 = Ind. Ant. 1881, p. 215). Thomas read the first part of the legend as ΣΑΝΑΒ or ΣΑΝΑΣ, and regarded the first three letters as an abbreviation of the word *saṃvatsara*, the fourth as the Greek numeral = 1, and the last as, perhaps, denoting some particular mint (JRAS. 1883, p. 75). C. read ΣΑΝΑΒ or ΣΑΝΑΟΒ, and ΚΟΡΡΑΝΟΥ or ΚΟΡΣΑΝΟΥ, comparing the legend of the oboli, which is distinctly ΜΙΑΟΥ ΚΟΡΣΑΝΟΥ, and translated 'the Kuṣana prince', supposing the first word to be the equivalent of a Scythic royal title *Tsanyu* or *Chanyu* = the title *devaputra* used by the Kuṣanas in their inscriptions (NChr. 1888, p. 47; 1890, p. 155). He also suggested that this Miaus may be the adventurer *Yin-mo-fu*, to whom the Chinese attribute the conquest of Kipin in B.C. 49 (REMUSAT, Nouv. Mélanges Asiat. I, p. 207; C.NChr. 1888, p. 51). The silver coins, tetradrachms and obols, bear legends in Gk. only. It is doubtful whether the attribution of a bilingual (Greek and Kharoṣṭhī) copper coin to Miaus (C.NChr. 1888, Pl. III, 13) can be supported. If so, its evidence would prove that Miaus ruled territory to the *south* of the Hindu Kush. This view is strengthened by the fact that all the obols were found in W. Afghanistan (C. op. cit. p. 50. For the opposite view, v. GARD. p. XLVIII and inf. § 36).

For the characteristic differences between the coins of Śakas and Kuṣanas, the discussion of which bears on the question of the nationality of Miaus, v. C.NChr. 1889, p. 294.

§ 36. The obols of Miaus are similar, both in fabric and in portraiture, to the coins of Hyrcodes (**Plate II, 2**), which seem undoubtedly not to have been struck on the Indian side of the Paropanisus, but to belong to the class of coins struck by the Kuṣanas or Yueh-ti in Bactria at some time subsequent to their settlement there c. 120 B.C. To the same class belong also the coins of Sapaleizes, which bear the name of the goddess Nannaia whose effigy so frequently occurs on the coins of the Kuṣanas — Kaniṣka, Huviṣka, and Vāsudeva.

C.NChr. 1889, p. 303; GARD. pp. XLVIII, 117, Pl. XXIV, 8—16.

§ 37. No adequate explanation has been given of the following:—

(1) The gold piece published in GARD. p. 162, Pl. XXIX, 15, and classed as Indo-Scythic, Uncertain. It is possible that this piece, which differs in important respects from all known coins, may be a reproduction in gold of the designs of two seals or gems.

(2) The thick piece of silver formerly belonging to General MALCOLM G. CLERK and now in the British Museum. This is said to have come from the Oxus country, and bears characters which have not yet been satisfactorily explained. It is possibly only a modern fabrication, or it may have been intended for use as a charm or ornament.

Proc. ASB. 1884, p. 127; id. 1885, p. 3.

§ 38. Indo-Chinese coins. — Copper coins found in the neighbourhood of Kashgar (J. R. Geogr. Soc. XLVII, p. 12) bearing inscrr. in both Indian (Kharoṣṭhī) and Chinese characters, show an extension to this region of some Indian power — perhaps Greek or Śaka. The Chinese inscrr. have reference to the weight or value of the coins. The Kharoṣṭhī inscrr. on the few known specimens are incomplete, but certainly contain fragments of the names of more than one ruler. All the suggested attributions of these coins to known Greek or Śaka kings are merely conjectural.

TERRIEN DE LACOUPERIE, Comptes rendus de l'Acad. des Inscrr. 1890, p. 338 (rev. Rev. Num. 1890, p. 256); GARD., NChr. 1879, p. 274 (appendix on geog., HOWORTH p. 279); GARD. p. 172, no. 4.

VI. COINS OF NATIVE INDIAN STATES FROM THE EARLIEST TIMES TO C. 50 A.D.

§ 39. This branch of Indian numismatics has only recently received any systematic treatment, and is still so full of difficulties, that the most convenient plan here will be to give in alphabetical order a list of those states whose earliest coins can, with any probability, be included within the wide limits given above.

§ 40. Almora. — There are three specimens, found near Almora, and now in the B. M., which are different in fabric from every other known Indian coinage. They appear to be of some alloy of silver and are heavier than any other Indian coins. Two of them bear in large Brāhmī characters, probably of a date between the 1st cent. B.C. and the 2nd cent. A.D., the names Śivadatta and Śivapāli[ta]. The *rev.* type — a Caitya-railing — is somewhat similar to that of some of the coins of Pañcāla (v. § 53) and on the *obv.* appears a Stag, as on the coins of the Kuṇindas (v. § 50).

PE. I, p. 224.

§ 41. Aparānta. — The legend on these coins has been read *Mahārājasa Apalātasa.* As they are similar in appearance to the coins struck by the Satraps of Mathurā (§ 32) and also by Hindu princes ruling in the same neighbourhood (v. inf. sub Mathurā § 52) their date is probably the latter part of the 1st cent. B.C. or the first part of the 1st cent. A.D.

C.CAI. p. 103; C.ASR. XIV, p. 136, Pl. XXXI, 3/ 4; PE. II, Pl. XLIV, 25. 26. For the locality of Aparānta = Northern Konkan: BHĀṆḌĀRKAR, Tr. I. Or. Congr. 1874, p. 313; and Hist. Dek. p. 17, note 4; C., however, CAI. p. 102, contends that Aparanta = W.Rajputana.

§ 42. Ārjunāyana (**Plate III, 20**). — The coins belong to the same class and period as the preceding. The Ārjunāyanas are mentioned in the Allahabad Pillar inscr. of Samudragupta (FLEET, CII. III, p. 8, and preface, p. 10).

C.CAI. p. 90, Pl. VIII, 20; PE. Pl. XLIV, 22.

§ 43. Audumbara or Odumbara (**Plate III, 8**). — The coins, found in the district of Pathānkot, are in style like the hemidrachms of the Greek prince Apollodotus and are found together with them. Their date is, therefore, probably c. 100 B.C. A similarity in style is also observable between the Audumbara coin given in C.CAI, Pl. IV, 1, and one of Azilises in NChr. 1890, Pl. X, 5a. Like their contemporaries the Kuṇindas (§ 50) the Audumbaras use both Brāhmī and Kharoṣṭhī coin-legends.

C.CAI. p. 66, Pl. IV; C.ASR. XIV, p. 115, Pl. XXXI, 1. 2; Proc. BA. 1885, p. 96; RODGERS, Cat. Lahore Mus. III, p. 151; SMITH, JBA. 1897, p. 8, Pl. I, 12.

§ 44. Ayodhyā.—The oldest coins seem to be the cast pieces (**Plate IV, 2**, and C.CAI. Pl. IX, 1—3), the date of which is, perhaps, before 200 B.C. The square inscribed pieces, most of which are also cast (**Plate IV, 4**, and id. 4—11), may belong to the 2nd cent. B.C. The other coins, which bear names ending in -mitra (**Plate IV, 3**, and id. 12—19, v. also SMITH, JRAS. 1889, p. 51) seem to belong to the same and following centuries. The relation of these Mitra coins to those found in N.Pañcāla, and the relation of either or both of these classes to the Śuṅga dynasty are at present matters of uncertainty (v. inf. § 53).

C.CAI. p. 90, Pl. IX; RIVETT-CARNAC, JBA. 1880, Pll. XVI. XVII; PE. I, p. 418, Pl. XXXIV, 19—21 etc.

§ 45. Bārān. — C. supposed this to be the ancient name of Bulandshahr and read the legend on the coins *Gomitasa Bārānāyā* (C.CAI. p. 88, Pl. VIII, 10; C.ASR. XIV, p. 147, Pl. XXXI, 15); but, as has been pointed out by BÜHLER, the old name of this place was *Varaṇa*, and the reading of the coin-legend is extremely doubtful. This Gomitra has usually been identified with one of the Hindu princes of Mathurā of the same name (v. inf. § 52); but the types of his coins are different and the forms of the Brāhmī letters of his coin-legends seem to be more ancient.

§ 46. Eraṇ—Erakina. — The coins found on the site of this ancient city in the Sāgar District are remarkable as being the finest specimens of purely native money (**Plate IV, 8**). It is possible to trace here the development of the *punch-mark* system into the *type* system. In the place of a number of symbols punched on to the coin from time to time, there appears at a later period a definite type, made up of a collection of these symbols struck from a die. This is usually the case in those parts of India which were least affected by foreign influence (cp. inf. § 129).

C.CAI. p. 99, Pl. XI; C.ASR. X, p. 77, Pl. XXIV, 15—17; id. XIV, p. 149, Pl. XXXI, 17. 18. For the reading of the legend of a very ancient coin from Eraṇ (Plate IV, 7), v. BÜHLER, Ind. Stud. III, p. 42; for other coins, of a later date, bearing the name of the city, v. C.ASR. X, l. c.

§ 47. Janapada. — No satisfactory explanation has yet been given of the coins which bear the legend *Rājña Janapadasa*, sometimes written in Brāhmī and sometimes in Kharoṣṭhī letters. C. suggests (loc. inf. cit.) that this may be a place-name = Rājasthān, or perhaps the name of the inhabitants of this place = the Χατριαῖοι, i. e. Kṣatriyas, of Ptolemy (VII, 1. 64; cp. L.IA. III, p. 141). To judge from style, the coins bearing an inscr. in Kharoṣṭhī characters (**Plate III, 18**) seem to belong to an earlier period than the others which are in fabric like the coins of the Satraps of Mathurā (**Plate III, 19**).

C.CAI. p. 89, Pl. VIII, 19; C.ASR. XIV, p. 151; PE. II, Pl. XLIV, 17—19.

§ 48. Kāḍa (**Plate III, 7**). — The attribution of the coins of cast copper, which bear the legend Kāḍasa in Brāhmī characters, is uncertain. BÜHLER explains Kāḍasa as the genitive of Kāḍa, the name of a king, a N.Indian form = Sk. *Kāla* or Pali *Kāḷa*, "black", and for the equation — N.Indian ḍ = Sk. l — compares forms found in the Girnār edicts, e. g. *mahiḍāyo* = Sk. *mahilāḥ* "women". The coin figured in C.CAI. Pl. V, 6, was found among coins of the Kuṇindas, and this fact led C. to conjecture that it may belong to the ancestors of the present Kaḍaik branch of the Kunets (C.CAI. p. 71; v. also § 50).

C.CAI. Pl. II, 21. 22; C.ASR. II, p. 10; VI, p. 167.

§ 49. Kosāmbī or Vatsa-pattana, an ancient city in the Allahabad District. (For its identification with the modern Kosam on the Jamna, and an outline of its history, v. C. Geog. p. 391.) The large cast coins which may be compared with those reading *Kāḍasa* (v. § 48) are probably as early as the 3rd cent. B.C. (**Plate III, 12**, cp. C.CAI. Pl. V, 7—10). The others (e. g. C., l. c. 11—18) may perhaps belong to the two following centuries. With them may be compared the coins of Pañcāla and the later coins of Ayodhyā (§§ 53. 44, and C.CAI. Pll. VII. IX). For the coins which bear the legend *Bahasatimitasa* (**Plate III, 11**) cp. the inscrr. of Bahasatimita at Pabhosā (FÜHRER, EI. II, p. 240).

C.CAI. p. 73, Pl. V, 7—18; C.ASR. I, p. 301; X, p. 4, Pl. II; PE. Pl. VIII, 12—15; JBA. 1873, pp. 109. 191.

§ 50. Kuṇinda. — The territory of the Kuṇindas would seem to be the hill districts, on both sides of the Satlej, occupied by the Kunets of the present day (C.ASR. XIV, 126). Their coins are of two periods. The earlier, which, like those of the Audumbaras, have legends in both Brāhmī and Kharoṣṭhī characters, and like them too are found in company with hemidrachms of Apollodotus (v. sup. § 43) are probably as early as B.C. 100 (**Plate III, 9**). The later, which seem to show the influence of the large copper money of the Kuṣanas, and which bear inscrr. in a later form of Brāhmī characters, may, perhaps, belong to the 3rd or 4th centuries, A.D. (**Plate III, 10**). The fact that the coins of the Yaudheyas also fall naturally into similar classes (§ 60) would seem to show that these Hindu states, and probably others, rose in power as the Greek and Kuṣana supremacies successively declined.

C.CAI. p. 70, Pl. V, 1—5; C.ASR. XIV, p. 137, Pl. XXXI, 5, 6; RODGERS, I. M. Cat. III, p. 9. Cp. also Ar. Ant. p. 413, Pl. XV, 23; PE. I, pp. 203. 208, Pl. XIX, 16; TH.JRAS. 1865, p. 447; JBA. 1875, p. 89; 1886, p. 161; Proc. BA. 1875, p. 164.

§ 51. Mālava. — The coins on which the legend *Mālavānāṃ Jayaḥ* has been read were formerly regarded as ancient; but both the character of their inscrr., and the fact that they are in fabric somewhat similar to the coins of the Nāgas of Padmāvatī (Smith, JRAS. 1897, p. 643; v. inf. § 101), point to a date not earlier than the 5th cent. A.D.

C.ASR. VI, pp. 165. 174; XIV, 149, Pl. XXXI, 19—25; Fleet, CII. III, Pref. p. 67; Rodgers, I. M. Cat. III, p. 15.

§ 52. Mathurā. — For an ancient cast coin found in the neighbourhood of Mathurā and bearing the inscr. *Upātikyā* in Brāhmī letters at least as early as the 3rd cent. B.C. (Plate III, 17) v. C.CAI. p. 86, Pl. VIII, 1; and C.ASR. III, pp. 14. 39. The coins of Balabhūti have Brāhmī characters of, probably, the 2nd cent. B.C. (C.CAI. p. 87, Pl. VIII, 9). For the coins of other Hindu princes found at Mathurā v. C.CAI. p. 88, Pl. VIII; and Bh.JRAS. 1894, p. 553, Pl. 10—14. Bh. assigns these to the period of the decline of Śaka power at Mathurā, i. e. after the last part of the 1st cent. B.C., thus assuming that they were imitated from the coins of the Śaka satraps of Mathurā (§ 32); but some of the coins of *Rāmadatta* (Plate IV, 1; C.CAI. Plate VIII, 13; and Bh.JRAS. 1894, Pl. 14) seem to be undoubtedly earlier, as they have for the reverse the incuse square which characterises the coins of Pañcāla (Śuṅgas, § 53). The coins of *Balabhūti* are also connected with those of *Bahasatimita* (§ 49) by identity of type — a Caitya-tree — and by their epigraphy. These considerations would seem to show that *some* at least of the Hindu princes preceded the Śaka satraps, who imitated their coins.

§ 53. Pañcāla (Plate III, 16). — The coins discussed under this heading have usually been attributed to the Śuṅga or Mitra dynasty, and it is by no means certain that they should not still be so classed. The difficulties affecting this identification are (1) the fact that most of the coins are found in Rohilkhand, the ancient kingdom of North Pañcāla, whereas other indications point to East Mālwa as the seat of Śuṅga power, (2) the fact that of the dozen names which occur on the coins, only one, that of Agnimitra, is found in the Śuṅga dynastic lists given in the Purāṇas. On the other hand, the *formation* of the names which generally end in *-mitra* is similar in either case; and the Śuṅga period, inferred from the Purāṇas, B.C. 176—66, is that of the style and epigraphy of the coins. There is probably, too, some connexion between these coins and the Mitra coins found at Ayodhyā (v. sup. § 44). These Pañcāla (Śuṅga) coins bear inscrr. in Brāhmī letters. For the characteristic features of their fabric, v. sup. § 52.

C.CAI. p. 79, Pl. VII; Carlleyle, JBA. 1880, p. 21; Rivett-Carnac, id. p. 87; Rājendra Lāla Mitra, Proc. BA. 1880, p. 8.

§ 54. Purī and Ganjam. — Numerous specimens of a peculiar class of bronze coins have been found in the Purī District of Orissa and in the neighbouring District of Ganjam in the Madras Presidency. They bear no inscriptions; but their types are evidently borrowed from those of the bronze Kuṣana coins of the time of Kaniṣka (§ 73) — viz. standing figure of the king on *obv.*, and the figure of some deity on *rev.* In the case of the chief recorded discovery of these coins in the Purī District, they were found in company with bronze Kuṣana coins struck in the ordinary manner. From this it would seem probable that the two classes — the struck originals and the cast imitations — were in circulation at the same time. It appears, however, to be a fact, that Kuṣana coins are not, as a rule, found so far east or south of India as Purī and Ganjam; and it has been suggested that their occurrence in these districts may be due to pilgrims who brought them from a distance as offerings at the shrines of Purī. It is, therefore, possible that the cast imitations in question may have been made for the same purpose, and that they should be regarded not as coins, but, like the *Rāma-*

ṭaṅkas of a later date, as temple-offerings. In either case they probably belong to that part of the Kuṣana period which lies between the reign of Kaniṣka and the end.

For the coins found in the Purī Dist., v. HOERNLÉ, Proc. ASB. 1895, p. 61, Pl. II; for those found in the Ganjam Dist., v. ELLIOT, Numismatic Gleanings p. 33 = JMLS. XX (New Series IV), p. 75.

§ 55. Sibi = the Sobii of Quintus Curtius (X, 4), the inhabitants of the country around Chitor. For coins on which this name has been read — in this case, however, the reading cannot be regarded as certain — v. C.ASR. VI, p. 204; XIV, p. 146, Pl. XXXI, 13. 14.

§ 56. Taxila, the modern Shāhdheri or Dheri Shāhān, in the Rāwal Pindi District (C. Geog. p. 104). For the coins of the earliest period, v. supra §§ 4—6. The art of striking from a die would seem to have been known here at an earlier period than elsewhere in India. The earliest specimens are struck only on one side, and by a method peculiarly Indian, according to which the metal was stamped while in a semi-molten state, with the result that the impress of the die was left enclosed in a deep incuse square. The coins of Pañcāla (§ 53) and Tripurī (§ 57) offer other examples of this method (BH.JRAS. 1894, p. 553). From the early square struck coins of Taxila (**Plate I, 11**) are imitated the copper coins of the Greek princes Pantaleon and Agathocles, c. 190, B.C. (**Plate I, 12**, Pantaleon). These, like all other Greek coins of the period, have types on both sides; and the 'double-die' coins of Taxila, the art of which, moreover, has an undoubtedly Greek appearance, are probably due to their influence (**Plate I, 13**). The double-die coins are succeeded by those of Maues, who probably conquered Taxila in the latter part of the 2nd cent. B.C. C. regards Liaka Kusuluka as a Śaka satrap of Maues at Taxila, interpreting the words of the Taxila copper-plate *Chaharā*[*ta*] *Cukhṣa* as one name = Taxila (Geog. p. 109).

C.CAI. p. 60, Pll. II. III; C.ASR. XIV, p. 16, Pl. X; Ar. Ant. Pl. XV, 26—31.

§ 57. Tripurī or Tripura, the ancient name of Tewar in the Jabalpur District (C.ASR. IX, p. 54). For the coins which bear this name in Brāhmī characters of, probably, the 3rd cent. B.C., v. BH.JRAS. 1894, p. 553, Pl. 15.

§ 58. Ujjain. — The earliest coins bear the inscr. *Ujeniya* in Brāhmī characters of probably the 2nd cent. B.C. (**Plate IV, 5**). All the other coins known at present are uninscribed, and are distinguished by a symbol which appears to be characteristic of, though not altogether confined to, this district (**Plate IV, 6**). They do not afford sufficient data to allow of any satisfactory chronological arrangement.

C.CAI. p. 94, Pl. X; C.ASR. XIV, p. 148, Pl. XXXI, 16; JBA. 1838, p. 1054, Pl. LXI, 2. 22.

§ 59. Vaṭasvaka (**Plate III, 6**). — The coins bearing this legend in Brāhmī characters similar to those on the square copper coins of Pantaleon and Agathocles (c. 190 B.C.) are also connected by identity of type with some of the 'single-die' coins found in the neighbourhood of Taxila (cp. C.CAI. Pl. II, no. 17 with no. 14). As coins of Pantaleon and Agathocles are imitated from these earlier single-die coins, the date of the Vaṭasvaka coins is probably at least as early as B.C. 200. BÜHLER has explained this name as denoting the Vaṭa (or Fig-tree) subdivision of the Aśvaka tribe (Ind. Stud. III, p. 46).

For the Aśvakas = Ἀσσακηνοί: Arrian, Anab. IV, 25, and Indica I, 1. Cp. also L.IA. II, p. 129; C.NChr. 1893, p. 100.

§ 60. Yaudheya. — The Yaudheyas have been identified with the modern Johiyas of Bhāwalpur (C. Geog. p. 245), but in ancient times their territory was more extended. The coins may be chronologically arranged as follows: (1) the smaller copper coins, which, though of rougher workmanship, may in other respects be compared with the earlier coins of the Audumbaras (§ 43) and Kuṇindas (§ 50) c. 100, B.C. (**Plate III**, 13); (2) the large copper coins, which show both in their fabric and in their types the influence of the Kuṣanas (**Plate III**, 14); the coins which have as their type a six-headed divinity, perhaps Kārttikeya, are somewhat later (**Plate III**, 15).

C.CAI. p. 75, Pl. VI; C.ASR. XIV, p. 139, Pl. XXXI, 7—12; PRINSEP, JBA. 1834, Pl. XXV, 4. 5; PE. Pl. IV, 11. 12; Pl. VII, 4; Pl. XIX, 5. 6. 9. 10. 22; Pl. XXI, 16. 17. The Yaudheyas tributary to Samudragupta: FLEET, CII. III, pp. 14. 251.

VII. INDO-PARTHIAN COINS.

§ 61. Date of I.-P. Dynasty. — The Indo-Parthian dynasty, the best-known member of which is *Gondophares*, seems to have succeeded the dynasty of Vonones in Kandahar and Seistan, and to have, at one period, extended its territories eastwards into the W.Panjab and Sind, which at an earlier date, formed the kingdom of Maues (v. sup. § 29; C.NChr. 1890, p. 122). With regard to the chronological limits — (1) the foundation of the dynasty seems to be after 1 B.C. (VON GUTSCH. Gesch. Ir. p. 134); and (2) the date of one of the latest kings, *Sanabares*, after 77 A.D. (VON SALLET, ZfN. 1879, p. 364). For a coin bearing the name of Aspavarma (v. sup. § 34), which seems to join in some manner as yet unexplained the two branches represented by Gondophares and Azes (§ 31) v. RODGERS, NChr. 1896, p. 268.

GARD., Parthian Coinage p. 46 (v. also DROUIN, Rev. Num. 1895, p. 46) makes Sanabares contemporary with Phraataces c. B.C. 3 — A.D. 4. This, however, depends on the reading of a date ΓΙΤ, Seleucid era 313 = A.D. 1, on a coin of Sanabares (TH. Sassanian Inscrr. 1868, p. 121); and MARKOFF, Zapiski Russian Asiatic Society 1892, p. 297 (v. also NChr. 1893, p. 218) has shown that this reading cannot be supported.

§ 62. Gondophares. — The date 21 A.D. as the first year of the reign Gondophares has been obtained from his Takht-i-Bahi inscr. by regarding the year 103 as Vikrama samvat.

C.NChr. 1890, p. 118; MARKOFF, Russ. As. Soc. 1892, p. 293, rev. DROUIN, Rev. Num. 1893, p. 119, and RAPSON, NChr. 1893, p. 217.

Whether this procedure be justifiable or not, the result well agrees with evidence derived from the epigraphy of the Greek legends of the coins (GARD. p. XLVI) and with other indications.

For the coins of this dynasty: GARD. p. 103, Pll. XXII. XXIII; VON SALLET, ZfN. 1880, p. 296; 1881, p. 111; C.NChr. 1890, p. 158, Pll. XIII. XIV; MARKOFF, op. cit. Pl. IV, 25—31; PE. II, p. 215. Coin of Abdagases with portion of Kharoṣṭhī inscr. written from left to right: HOERNLE, Proc. BA. 1895, p. 83. For the identification of Gondophares with the Gundophorus of the apocryphal Acts of St. Thomas: VON GUTSCH., N. Rhein. Mus. f. Philol. XIX, p. 161; cp. also Gesch. Ir. p. 134; GARD. p. XLIII; PE. II, p. 214.

§ 63. Wrongly attributed coins. — The term *Indo-Parthian* has also been applied by TH. (JRAS. 1870, p. 503 = NChr. 1870, p. 139 = with additions, ASWI. 1874—75 "Kāṭhiāwāḍ and Kacch", p. 52 = Dynasty of Guptas &c. p. 37) to certain thin coins of Sassanian fabric, which are more probably to be attributed to some dynasty — perhaps the Ephthalites or their Turkish conquerors — reigning in territory to the north of India and at a period not earlier than the middle of the 6th cent. A. D.

RAPSON, NChr. 1896, p. 246. Cp. also MARKOFF, Russ. As. Soc. 1892, p. 298, Pl. IV, 32. 33 (rev. Rev. Num. 1893, p. 130; and NChr. 1893, p. 219). For the epigraphy: DROUIN, JA. 1891 (XVII), p. 148 = Rev. Num. 1891, p. 222.

VIII. KUṢANA COINS.

§ 64. Definition. — As considerable confusion has sometimes arisen from an inaccurate use of the term 'Kuṣana', it should be borne in mind that it bears two distinct significations, according to the period of which it is used: — (1) the Kuṣanas were originally one of the five tribes of the Yueh-ti, who, by c. 120 B.C., had become the predominant power in Bactria and other neighbouring countries to the north of the Paropanisus; (2) c. 25 B.C., this particular tribe gained a supremacy over the other four tribes of Yueh-ti, and, from this time onwards, the word 'Kuṣana' is used to denote the whole Yueh-ti people united under their leadership. The first result of this unity of the previously separate and, perhaps, somewhat discordant forces of the Yueh-ti, was the conquest of the last remaining Greek kingdom in the Kabul valley under Hermaeus.

SPECHT, JA. 1883 (II), p. 317; TH., Ind. Ant. 1886, p. 19; C.NChr. 1889, p. 269; 1892, p. 41. But see S. LÉVI, JA. 1897, p. 1 ff.

§ 65. Hermaeus, Kujula Kadphises. — The numismatic evidence of the progress of this Kuṣana conquest of the kingdom of Hermaeus is complete. The coins show the following sequence: — (1) Hermaeus alone (GARD. p. 62); (2) Kujula Kadphises associated with Hermaeus, i. e. *obv.* ΕΡΜΑΙΟΥ, *rev.* in Kharoṣṭhī *Kujula Kasasa* (Plate II, 7; cp. GARD. p. 120); (3) Kujula Kadphises alone, i. e. *obv.* ΚΟΖΟΥΛΟ ΚΑΔΦΙΖΟΥ, *rev. Kujula Kasasa* (Plate II, 8; cp. GARD. p. 122). Kujula Kadphises (= Kieu-tsieu-khio in Chinese) is said to have died at the age of 80, c. A.D. 10, and the conquest of India, i. e. the Panjab and the territory as far as the Jamna is ascribed to his successor (SPECHT, JA. 1883 (II), p. 325).

DROUIN, Rev. Num. 1888, p. 23; C.NChr. 1892, p. 45, puts the date of Kujula Kadphises rather later, viz. c. B.C. 10, and regards Hima Kadphises as having immediately succeeded him, c. A.D. 30. For the Greek inscr. on coins of Hermaeus and Kujula Kadphises, v. RAPSON, JRAS. 1897, p. 319.

§ 66. There is less certainty in regard to the coins which should be attributed to this second prince of the Kuṣana dynasty. By many writers he is identified with the prince whose coins, directly imitated from the denarii of Augustus of the years 4 B.C. — 2 A.D. (VON SALLET, ZfN. 1879, p. 378) are inscribed, *obv.* ΚΟΖΟΛΑ ΚΑΔΑΦΕϹ, *rev. Kuyula Kaphsasa* (Plate II, 9); cp. VON GUTSCH., Gesch. Ir. p. 136; GARD. p. XLVIII; DROUIN, Rev. Num. 1888, p. 46). C., however, supposes these coins of Roman type to be the issue of some particular mint of Kujula Kadphises, and explains the differences in the inscriptions as due to the difficulty of representing a Kuṣana name in either Greek or Kharoṣṭhī characters (NChr. 1892, p. 46).

§ 67. The Nameless King. — This will, perhaps, be the most fitting place to discuss the attribution of the coins of 'the Nameless King', whose legends afford us only such information as is conveyed by the title ΒΑϹΙΛΕΥϹ ΒΑϹΙΛΕΥΩΝ (sic) ϹΩΤΗΡ ΜΕΓΑϹ, rarely accompanied by a Kharoṣṭhī translation (Plate II, 10; cp. GARD. p. 114). The extent of his dominion is shown by the fact that his coins are found in great numbers "all over the Panjab, as well as in Kandahar, and in the Kabul valley" (C.NChr. 1890, p. 115). From a consideration of the fabric and epigraphy of these coins certain tangible facts are deducible. They are connected, on the one hand, with those of Miaus (§ 35), by similarity of type, *rev.* Horseman, and by the use of the "reel and bead" border (cp. Pl. II, 1 with 10; C.NChr. 1890, Pl. XII, 1 with 4; GARD. Pl. XXIV, 7 with 6); and, on the other hand, with those of Hima Kadphises (§ 69), by the use of the nominative instead of the more usual genitive in the Greek inscriptions, by the use of the title σωτὴρ μέγας, and by the similarity in form between certain letters both in the Greek and Kharoṣṭhī inscrr. (C.NChr. 1892, p. 71). Moreover, the Nameless King uses a symbol of the kind which is characteristic of Hima Kadphises and his successors; and, on a unique coin, published by C. (NChr. 1892, Pl. V, 14) there occurs a bust with two faces, and, in front of the faces, the symbols respectively of the Nameless King and Hima Kadphises (C.NChr. 1892, p. 71). It cannot be doubted that these two were nearly related in point of time; whether they were also connected as members of the same dynasty is not so certain. C. places the Nameless King among the Śakas (NChr. 1890, p. 114), but also suggests that these coins without a name may have been issued by the satraps of one of the early Kuṣana kings, perhaps of Hima Kadphises himself. von Gutschmid (Gesch. Ir. p. 136), recognising the numismatic break which occurs between Kozola Kadaphes and the later Hima Kadphises, places the Nameless King in the interval, and regards him as an Indian prince — the Āgniveśya prince, who, according to the Gārgī Saṃhitā (Kern, Bṛhat-Saṃhitā 39) ruled over India for 20 years between two Śaka dynasties. C., too, saw the feasibility of some such view and suggested that the Kharoṣṭhī *Vi*, which occurs on many of these coins (e. g. C.NChr. 1890, Pl. XII, 4) might be an abbreviation of *Vikramâditya* (l. c. p. 115). It must be pointed out, however, that, if any such identification of the Nameless King with Vikramāditya is possible, the Vikrama era, which begins with 57 B.C., must, if our chronology of this period is correct, be supposed to date from his birth.

§ 68. Kujula Kara Kadphises. — This prince, who bears the Kuṣana title *Devaputra*, is supposed by C. to be the son of Kujula Kadphises, and the predecessor of Hima Kadphises.

NChr. 1892, p. 65, Pl. IV, 9—13. In the chronological table on p. 45, he is, however, placed after Hima Kadphises and before Kaniṣka.

Usually, however, it has been assumed that the coins bearing this form of the name are merely varieties of the coinage of Kujula Kadphises (v. sup. § 65); and, in favour of this assumption which allows them an earlier date, it may be pointed out that in type and execution they somewhat resemble those of Zeionises (v. sup. § 34; cp. Gard. Pl. XXIII, 5, Zeionises, with 7, Kujula Kara Kadphises).

§ 69. Hima Kadphises. — The order of succession of the Indian Kuṣana monarchs from this point to the last quarter of the 2nd cent. A.D. is certain. *Hima Kadphises* who has been identified with the Yen-kao-ching of the Chinese accounts (c. 30—78 A.D.; **Plate II, 11**) is connected with his successors as the first to issue the gold coinage, which is continued by the Guptas after the supremacy of Northern India had passed into their hands in the 4th cent. A.D. With the exception of two or three gold coins of Eucratides (Rev. Num. 1867, p. 382; NChr. 1892, p. 37, Pl. III, 11), one of Menander (C. coll., now in B.M.) and, perhaps, one of Taxila (C.CAI. Pl. II, 18), and another coin of uncertain attribution (Gard. p. 162, Pl. XXIX, 15, v. sup. § 37 (1)), no specimens which can possibly have been struck in India, during the two centuries previous to the date of Hima Kadphises, are to be found in the collections of the present day. The large gold coinage of the Kuṣanas has been attributed to the influx of Roman gold to India at this period.

C.NChr. 1888, p. 219, and the passage of Pliny there quoted, Hist. Nat. XII, 41 (18).

§ 70. Certain it is that the Roman weight-standard (*aureus* = 124 grains or 8,035 grammes) was adopted in India at this time. Pieces of the weight of two aurei were only struck by Hima Kadphises; the largest gold coins of his successors are aurei.

For a table of the weights of these and later Kuṣana gold coins, v. C.CMI. p. 16.

§ 71. The coin-legends of Hima Kadphises are both in Greek and Kharoṣṭhī. Those of his three next successors are in Greek only. Afterwards, Nāgarī letters and monograms are used instead of the Greek inscriptions which had ceased to be intelligible (v. inf. § 74).

For coins of Hima Kadphises with unusual Kharoṣṭhī inscrr., v. HOERNLE, Proc. BA. 1895, p. 82.

§ 72. **Kaniṣka, Huviṣka, Vāsudeva.** — The Śaka era has usually been supposed to date from the *abhiṣeka* of *Kaniṣka* at Mathurā in 78 A.D. (OLDENBERG, ZfN. 1881, p. 292 = Ind. Ant. 1881, p. 214); and to this era the dates found in the stone inscrr. of *Kaniṣka*, *Huviṣka*, and *Vāsudeva*, have usually been referred. If this supposition be correct, the known dates will be as follows: — Kaniṣka, years 7—28 = A.D. 85—106; Huviṣka, years 33—64 = A.D. 111—142; Vāsudeva, years 74—98 = A.D. 152—176.

C.NChr. 1892, p. 49. It used to be supposed that Vāsudeva's inscriptional dates began much earlier, so as to make the first part of his reign coincident with the last part of Huviṣka's (cp. GARD. p. LI; DROUIN, Rev. Num. 1888, p. 38); but C. (l. c.) suggests that this may be due to a misreading of the decimal figure 70 as 40. Coins of Huviṣka with inscrr. in Brāhmī characters: SMITH, JBA. 1897, p. 3.

C., however, reasoning from the fact that Kaniṣka was a Kuṣana and *not* a Śaka king (v. sup. § 64), seeks another origin for the Śaka era (he supposes it to have been founded by Caṣṭana, v. inf. § 80), and explains the Kuṣana dates as being of the Seleucid era (B.C. 312), with the hundreds omitted (e. g. year 7 = 407 Seleucid = 95 A.D.). This procedure would make all the Kuṣana dates, as given above, 10 years later. C. justifies it by referring to the fact that the Kuṣanas use the Macedonian, and not the Indian, names of the months in their inscrr. (NChr. 1892, p. 44); compare also BHĀṆḌĀRKAR (Hist. Dek. p. 26 f.). Regarding another possibility, viz. that the dates of Kaniṣka and his successors have to be referred to the second century of the era, used by Śoḍāsa, Liako Kusuluka and others, see WZKM. IX, p. 173 f.

§ 73. **Religious emblems.** — As illustrating the religious history of this period, the coins of Kaniṣka and Huviṣka are important. They show a remarkable eclecticism; for on their reverses are represented Greek and Scythic divinities, deities of the Avesta and of the Vedas, and Buddha.

For the coins of the Early Great Kuṣanas: C.NChr. 1892, p. 63, Pll. IV—VIII; id. p. 98, Pll. IX—XIV; GARD. pp. XLVIII, 120, Pll. XXV—XXIX; VON SALLET, ZfN. 1879, p. 377. Cp. also Ar. Ant. p. 347, Pl. X. For the chronology: DROUIN, Rev. Num. 1888, pp. 8. 185; VON GUTSCH., Gesch. Ir. pp. 136. 164. Kuṣana modifications of the Greek alphabet: STEIN, Baby. and Or. Rec. 1887, p. 155; C. id. 1888, p. 40. Divinities represented on the coins: STEIN op. c. = Ind. Ant. 1888, p. 89; C.NChr. 1892, pp. 61. 128; TH. JRAS. 1877, p. 209; HOFFMANN, Abh. f. d. K. des Morg. 1881, p. 139; GARD. p. LX; RAPSON, JRAS. 1897, p. 322, for the reading OHÞO as a name of Śiva.

§ 74. **Later Great Kuṣanas.** — After the death of Vāsudeva, c. 180 A.D., the gold and copper coinage of the Kuṣanas continues, but the Greek inscrr. no longer afford any information. They are mechanically repeated and rapidly become debased and illegible. Two or three isolated Nāgarī letters or monograms are usually found on the reverse of the coins. These were, no doubt, at the time, significant abbreviations, but all hope for their interpretation now lies in further discoveries of inscrr. of this period. These coins probably constituted the currency of both the Kabul Valley and the Panjab during the long period from 180 A.D. to c. 425 A.D., the date of the settlement of Kidāra Shāh in Gandhāra (§ 76). Within these limits the relative age of different classes may be determined by their nearness to or remoteness from the originals from which they were copied. Thus C.'s class A (NChr. 1893, p. 115, Pl. VIII) on which the names of Kaniṣka or Vāsudeva can still be read, is, no doubt, older than his class B (id. p. 120, Pl. IX) on which only a few vestiges of the Greek letters remain. A criterion of locality may also be applied:—(1) the coins bearing OHÞO on the *rev.*, with type, Śiva and his bull Nandi (**Plate II, 13**) derived from the earlier Kuṣana types of Vāsudeva (**Plate II, 12**) belong rather to the Kabul Valley: they were imitated by the Scytho-Sassanians (§ 75); (2) those with APΔOXÞO, and type, seated goddess (**Plate II, 14**), belong rather to the more eastern portion of the Kuṣana dominions: they were imitated by the Kidāra Kuṣanas (§ 76) and by the Guptas (§ 91; C.NChr. 1893, p. 115 — by an error in his mode of statement, he seems to mean the opposite). This type is probably also derived from the earlier Kuṣanas (e. g. GARD. Pl. XXVI, 18: Kaniṣka). This is, however, not certain, as all the coins attributed to the earlier Kuṣanas which bear this type have a late appearance, and it is possible that they may all have been struck by the later Great Kuṣanas who mechanically repeated the names of their predecessors in the Greek inscrr. on the *obv.*

C.NChr. 1893, p. 112, Pll. VIII—X. Cp. also TH., Ind. Ant. 1883, p. 6; SMITH, JBA. 1897, p. 3. For a coin which seems to combine a Kuṣana *obv.* with a Sassanian *rev.*, v. SMITH, op. cit. p. 5.

§ 75. Scytho-Sassanians. — These coins come generally from the districts on the Oxus, to the north of the Paropanisus; but, as they are also occasionally found in the Kabul Valley and are, probably, the result of invasions into this district (§ 115), they call for a short notice here (**Plate II, 15**). Their limits of date are approximately fixed by the following data:—(1) Some of the earliest specimens bear the head-dress and name of the Sassanian king, Hormazd II (A.D. 301—310), who married a daughter of the Kuṣana king of Kabul; (2) the later limit (A.D. 450) marks the date at which the territories on the Oxus were wrested from the Sassanians by the Ephthalites (C.NChr. 1893, p. 169). The date of the different coins is, in most cases, fixed, as they usually bear the head-dress of the contemporary Sassanian monarch, together with his name and titles in a debased form of the Greek alphabet.

C.NChr. 1893, p. 166, Pl. XIII. XIV.

According to this view this class of coins was issued by Sassanian conquerors of the Yueh-ti whose territory lay to the north of the Paropanisus.

Another view is that of DROUIN who regards them as coins of the Yueh-ti (Kuṣanas) themselves, and explains the occurence of Sassanian names and head-dresses, by supposing that both were borrowed by these Yueh-ti as a consequence of their long friendly alliance with the Sassanian monarchy. According to this view, therefore, these coins are of the Later Great Kuṣanas; and are distinguished from those treated of in § 74 only as being the issue of a different district comprising a portion of the extreme north of India and also Arachosia and Bactriana on the other side of the Paropanisus.

DROUIN, Rev. Num. 1896, p. 154, Pl. V.

§ 76. Kidāra or Little Kuṣanas. — From Chinese sources (SPECHT, JA. 1883 (II), p. 328) we learn that Ki-to-lo, the leader of the Great Yueh-ti, who has been identified by C. (NChr. 1893, p. 184) with the Kidāra of the coins, being hard pressed by the Ephthalites, crossed over the Paropanisus and established in Gandhāra — the Kabul Valley and Panjab — the kingdom of the Little Yueh-ti. The date of this invasion is approximately fixed at A.D. 425, as the Ephthalites, some time afterwards, sustained a signal defeat at the hands of Varahrān V, A.D. 428. The other limit, 475 A.D., marks the conquest of Gandhāra by the Ephthalites. The Kidāra Kuṣanas seem to have retired "to the north, into Chitral and Gilgit to the west of the Indus, and to Pakhali and Kashmir to the east of the river" (C.NChr. 1893, p. 187). Their power can be traced in the coinage of Kashmir (§ 112), and their kingdom was again established on the Upper Indus after the defeat of the Hūṇa Mihirakula (v. inf. § 107), and lasted until, in the 9th cent. A.D., a revolution placed a Brāhman dynasty on the throne (v. inf. § 115). The coins of the Kidāra Kuṣanas have as their *rev.* type the seated goddess, which characterises class (2) of the coins of the later Great Kuṣanas (§ 74). This fact suggests their attribution to Kashmir rather than to Gandhāra. They bear on the *obv.* the name Kidāra, the founder of the dynasty, and on the *rev.* the name of the ruling sovereign (Plate II, 16).

C.NChr. 1893, p. 184, Pl. XV; Proc. BA. 1888, p. 205. For the chronology and ethnology: DROUIN, JA. 1891, (XVII), p. 146 = Rev. Num. 1891, p. 219; HE. p. 14, from the Muséon, 1895; GUTSCH., Gesch. Ir. p. 168.

IX. DYNASTIES CONTEMPORARY WITH THE KUṢANAS.

§ 77. Now that we have traced the coinages of the Kuṣanas down to a period where the inroads of the Hūṇas (Ephthalites or White Huns) make a conspicuous land-mark in the history of India, it will be a convenient opportunity to return and describe the coinages of other powers contemporary with the Kuṣanas.

§ 78. Kṣaharātas. — This is probably the name of some Śaka family or tribe. The evidence is as follows:—(1) on the Taxila copper-plate grant of the 78th year of the Great King Moga (v. sup. § 29), Patika is described as the son of Liaka Kusuluka, satrap of the Chaharā[ta] and Cukhṣa (tribes);

BH.JRAS. 1894, p. 551, the tribal names corrected in accordance with DOWSON's original reading (JRAS. 1863, p. 221) since verified by BÜHLER. For C.'s interpretation of these two words, v. sup. § 56.

(2) the Lion Capital, in which mention is made of the Great Satrap Kusulaa, is dedicated 'for the worship of the whole of Śakasthāna' (BH. ed BÜHLER, JRAS. 1894, p. 540);

(3) Nahapāna is described as a *Kṣaharāta* (Brāhmī) = *Chahaṛata* (Kharoṣṭhī) on his coins (BH.JRAS. 1890, p. 642, Pl. I), and known as a Śaka from the inscrr. of his son-in-law Uṣavadāta (C.CAI. p. 105; ASWI. IV, p. 101);

(4) Nahapāna's conqueror, the Āndhra Śatakarṇi, boasts of having defeated the Śakas and of having entirely uprooted the Khakharāta family (OLD., ZfN. 1881, p. 320 = Ind. Ant. 1881, p. 226; ASWI. IV, p. 108).

§ 79. Nahapāna. — There is no sufficient ground for the identification either of Liaka Kusuluka with the Kuṣana Kozola Kadaphes (GARD. p. XLIX), or of Kṣaharāta with the Kharamosta of the coins (C.NChr. 1890, p. 171) or the Kharaosta of the Lion Capital (BH.JRAS. 1890, p. 641; 1894, p. 549). There are, therefore, no coins, known at present which can, with any certainty, be attributed to this family except those of *Nahapāna* (Plate III, 1), the satrap who ruled over the southernmost conquests of the Śakas including "a portion of the Deccan or Marāṭha country, the northern Konkan, some portion of Gujarāt proper, and Surāṣtra or Kāṭhiāwāḍ and Kacch." (BH.JRAS. 1890, p. 642). Some of these territories were conquered from the Andhras

(v. inf. § 86), and it has been conjectured by Bh. that the initial year of the Śaka era marks the date of this Śaka victory.

L. c. For other views as to the origin of this era, v. §§ 72. 80; C.CMI. p. 3, refers the dates of Nahapāna's inscrr. to the era of the Mālavas, or Vikramāditya saṃvat, B.C. 57.

In turn, however, Nahapāna was certainly defeated by the Andhras, and another family of satraps, probably at first acknowledging the supremacy of the Andhra king, takes the place of the Kṣaharātas.

Oldenberg, ZfN. 1881, p. 322 = Ind. Ant. 1881, p. 225; Bühler, Ind. Ant. 1883, p. 272; Bhaṇḍārkar, Hist. Dek. p. 25.

§ 80. Kṣatrapas of Surāṣṭra. — The first member of this family, whom C. regards as the founder of the Śaka era (CMI. p. 3) was *Caṣṭana* (Plate III, 2), who was, probably, for some time contemporary with Nahapāna, and, perhaps, had like him a Śaka origin.

Bh.JRAS. 1890, p. 644, wrongly reading *Cutsa* instead of *Cukhsa* on the Taxila copper-plate (v. sup. § 33) sees in this tribal name the origin of the name Caṣṭana.

His territory would seem to have been originally in W.Rajputana, and subsequently to have included Mālwa (capital Ujjain).

Bh.JRAS. 1890, p. 644; Bhaṇḍ., Hist. Dek. p. 28.

After Nahapāna, the territory of these satraps probably embraced the districts originally governed by Nahapāna and Caṣṭana separately. The suzerainty of the Andhras was, apparently, alternately successfully disputed and reasserted during the reigns of the first two satraps, Caṣṭana and Jayadāman. The distinction between the titles mahākṣatrapa and kṣatrapa on these earliest coins may be thus explained — Caṣṭana originally a simple kṣatrapa becomes a mahākṣatrapa, while his successor bears only the inferior title (Bh.JRAS. 1890, p. 645). The independence of this dynasty seems to have been permanently established by the third satrap, *Rudradāman*, who boasts, in his Junāgaḍh inscr., of having twice conquered the Sātakarṇi king of the Deccan, and of having won for himself the title of mahākṣatrapa (*svayamabhigata-mahākṣatrapanāmnaḥ*). After the time of Rudradāman, as is proved by the coin-dates, the reigning sovereign is regularly styled mahākṣatrapa; and the the heir apparent, who governed some portion of the kingdom as viceroy, is styled kṣatrapa.

§ 81. Coins of the W.Kṣatrapas. — The silver coins both of Nahapāna and of Caṣṭana and his successors are copied from the hemidrachms of the Greek princes of the Panjab — more particularly, perhaps, from those of Apollodotus Philopator (C.CMI. p. 3) and seem to follow the same weight-standard (the Persian, v. sup. § 8: hemi-drachm = 43,2 grains or 2,8 grms.). Traces of this origin are to be seen in the fragmentary inscr. in Greek characters, which still continued to be repeated as a sort of ornament on the *obv.* of the satrap coins after its significance was lost.

For attempts to explain these Greek letters as significant v. Th.JRAS. 1850, p. 52; Bh., id. 1890, pp. 643. 648; PE. II, p. 88.

The coins of Caṣṭana, like those of Nahapāna, bear inscrr. in Nāgarī and Kharoṣṭhī characters: on all subsequent coins Nāgarī inscrr. only are found. The coinage throughout this period is chiefly of silver, but specimens in billon and copper are also known (e. g. C.CMI. Pl. I, 7—12).

§ 82. Inscrr. on Kṣatr. Coins. — The long *rev.* inscrr. regularly give the names and titles both of the reigning satrap and of his father. The data thus afforded, when taken in conjunction with the dates on the *obv.* (v. inf. § 83), make it possible to reconstruct the outlines of this dynasty with an unusual degree of precision (v. Genealogical Table in C.CMI. p. 5). An interloper, named Īsvaradatta, who takes the title *mahākṣatrapa* and strikes coins dated in the first and second years of his own reign, is probably to be placed between the fourteenth and fifteenth members of the dynasty, Vijayasena and Dāmajaḍasrī III (v. inf. § 84).

There is a coin of an otherwise unknown Kṣatrapa, Satyadāman son of Dāmajaḍaśrī I, in the collection of Col. J. BIDDULPH. This coin is remarkable as having its inscr. in pure Sanskrit. For a coin of Arjuna, who may possibly also be a member of this dynasty, v. SMITH, JBA. 1897, p. 9, Pl. I, 15.

§ 83. Dates on Kṣatr. Coins. — The inscriptional dates begin with the year 72 of Rudradāman's Junāgaḍh inscr. (v. sup. § 80). The coin-dates (Plate III, 3; Dāmasena, date 153) begin with the year 100, in the reign of the 5th satrap, Jīvadāman, and continue regularly to the end of the dynasty. The last known dates are those of Rudrasiṃha, 310, and of his sister's son Siṃhasena, 304 (BH.JRAS. 1890, p. 662; C.CMI. p. 4). In determining the era to which these dates should be referred, it should be borne in mind that they probably do not mark the extreme limits of the dynasty. In the period of confusion, when the kingdom of the satraps was falling to pieces before the attacks of the Guptas, it is at least possible that no coins may have been struck. The earliest coins of the Guptas struck in this part of India have, unfortunately, no dates which have as yet been read with certainty (SMITH, JRAS. 1889, p. 123); but it is certain that the Gupta conquest took place in the latter part of the reign of Candragupta Vikramāditya (c. A.D. 380—414, SMITH, JRAS. 1893, p. 82). If, therefore, the coin-dates of these satraps be referred to the Saka era, 78 A.D., the latest known date 310 = A.D. 388, would fall well within the reign of Candragupta; and there would seem to be no sufficient reason for the alternative which has been suggested by OLDENBERG (ZfN. 1881, p. 318 = Ind. Ant. 1881, p. 224), viz. that these dates should be referred to an independent satrapal era beginning c. 100 A.D.

Cp. also Ar. Ant. p. 405; STEVENSON, JBRA. II, p. 377; NEWTON, id. 1861, p. 15; VII, p. 1; IX, p. 1; TH.JRAS. 1850, p. 1; FLEET, Ind. Ant. 1885, p. 325; PE. I, pp. 334. 425; II, pp. 69. 84. For the numerals, cp. also PE. II, p. 80; BHAU DĀJĪ, JBRA. VIII, p. 225.

§ 84. Ābhīras. — These Ābhīra kings are known from inscrr. at Nasik, and also from the Pauranic lists (BHAṆḌ., Hist. Dek. p. 45; Tr. I. Or. Cong. 1874, p. 341; BÜHLER, ASWI. IV, 103 f.). They are known to have been connected with the Kṣatrapas of Surāṣṭra and Malwa sometimes as commanders of their armies (BH.JRAS. 1890, p. 657); and it has been suggested that they were the governors of the Sahyādris and Konkan during the same period (BH., Bomb. Gaz. XVI, p. 624). It has been conjectured that the interruption in the line of Mahākṣatrapas between Vijayasena, year 171, and Dāmajaḍaśrī, year 176 (v. sup. § 82), may have been caused by an insurrection of the Ābhīra king against his feudal lord. The contemporary Kṣatrapa, Vīradāman reigns uninterruptedly through this interval, but the position of Mahākṣatrapa seems to have been usurped by Īśvaradatta who strikes coins apparently imitated from those both of Vijayasena and Vīradāman dated in the first and second years of his reign. This conjecture is supported by arguments derived from (1) the formation of the name, and (2) the method of dating in regnal years.

BH.JRAS. 1890, p. 656. BH. points out that if the last year of Vijayasena, 171, be the first year of Īśvaradatta, this = 248 A.D. may possibly mark the beginning of the Trikūṭaka (or of the Chedi) era; v. also C.CMI. p. 4. He also suggests that Mādharīputa, who is usually regarded as an Andhra may be an Ābhīra. The use of metronymics is common to Andhras and Ābhīras (Bomb. Gaz. XVI, p. 623, note 2).

§ 85. The Andhras. — The Andhras (Andhrabhṛtyas or Sātavāhanas), though classed by the Purāṇas among the rulers of Magadha, are, in historical times, a Southern Indian power, the capital of which was Dhānyakaṭaka = Dharanikot or Amarāvatī on the Kistna in the Gantur Dist. of Madras (C., Geog. p. 540). But as, during the period for which the evidence of coins is available, their history is closely connected with that of the Kṣaharātas and the Kṣatrapas of Surāṣṭra and Malwa, and as the style of some of the coins themselves bears witness to this fact, it will be most convenient to discuss them here.

§ 86. E. and W. Andhras. — At some time previous to this period the Andhra kingdom had been extended westwards across the peninsula from sea to sea, and northwards beyond the Narbadda. The provinces to the north of this river seem to have been conquered by Nahapāna (BH.JRAS. 1890, p. 642), reconquered by *Gotamīputra Sātakarṇi I* (prob. beg. of 2nd cent. A.D.), and included in the satrapy of Caṣṭana. Of this western and northern portion of the Andhra kingdom, the capital was Paithan, the ancient Pratiṣṭhāna, on the Godavari in the Aurangabad Dist. of the Nizam's Dominions. It has been supposed (BHAṆḌ., Hist. Dek. p. 33) that at this second capital the heir apparent to the throne ruled as viceroy, bearing the same relation to the Andhra sovereign at Dhānyakaṭaka as the *kṣatrapa* bore to the *mahākṣatrapa* in the kingdom of Surāṣṭra and Malwa after the time of Rudradāman. This point is not determined by the coin-legends; but it is noteworthy that the two chief classes of Andhra coins correspond to these two divisions of the kingdom. The same names are found on the coins of both classes; but the Western coins, found chiefly in the state of Kolhapur, are distinguished from the Eastern, found chiefly in the deltas of the Godavari and Kistna, not only by their types (C.CAI. p. 107), but also by the fact that their inscrr. include certain names or titles not found on the others.

Viḷivāyakurasa on coins of Gotamīputa (Plate III, 4) and Vāsiṭhīputa, and *Sevalakurasa* (BHAṆḌ., Hist. Dek. p. 20) or *Sivāla°* (C.) on coins of Māḍharīputa. BHAṆḌ. (l. c.) interprets these as names of viceroys of the Kolhapur dist. He supposes the former to be mentioned by Ptolemy VII, 1, 83: Ἱππόκουρα (=? Karhāḍ or Kolhapur, p. 44) Βασίλειον Βαλεοκούρου.

§ 87. Types of E. and W. Andhra coins. — From a consideration of the types represented on the coins of these two classes, the following suggestions may be made: — (1) the 'caitya' symbol which is characteristic of the coins of Caṣṭana and all his successors is no doubt derived from the Andhras; (2) the use of the symbol found on most of the coins of Ujjain seems to be an additional piece of evidence of the fact that, before the Saka conquest under Nahapāna, Malwa was included in the Andhra dominions; (3) the style and types of other coins seem to connect them with coins ascribed to the Pallavas (v. inf. § 128).

All the Andhra coins hitherto mentioned are of lead or of a peculiar alloy of copper; in fabric they differ greatly from the northern coinages; and nothing certain can be said about their weight-standard; but compare E.CSI. p. 23, note 2.

There is, however, a third class, a specimen of which was discovered in the tope at Supāra, which is of silver, precisely similar in fabric and style to the earliest coins of the Kṣatrapas of Surāṣṭra and Malwa, and probably struck according to the same weight-standard (Plate III, 5). Of this coinage only two specimens are at present known, and both of them bear the name of *Siriyaña Gotamīputa Sātakaṇi II*, who may, perhaps, have been a contemporary of Jayadāman or Rudradāman.

BH.JBRA. XV, p. 305, Pl. II, 7. 7a; BÜHLER, Ind. Ant. 1883, p. 273.

§ 88. Succession of Andhra kings. — In regard to the order of succession and chronological arrangement of the different members of this dynasty there is at present great uncertainty, and this uncertainty extends to the attribution of the coins. Those bearing the inscr. *Raño Gotamīputasa Viḷivāyakurasa* (C.CAI. Pl. XII, 6. 7; E.CSI. Pl. II, 39. 40) are by some (BHAND., Tr. I. Or. Cong. 1874, p. 351; OLD., Ind. Ant. 1881, p. 226) assigned to Gotamīputra Sātakarṇi I, the conqueror of Nahapāna, and by others (BH. JBRA. XIII, p. 308; C.CAI. p. 105) to Siriyaña Gotamīputa Sātakaṇi II, whose name occurs in full on other issues (§ 87; C.CAI. Pl. XII, 8—12; E.CSI. p. 25). The attribution of the coins of the successor of Gotamīputa Sātakaṇi I, *Vāsiṭhīputa Puḷumāyi*, who was probably contemporary with Caṣṭana, is, on the other hand, quite certain[1].

There is less certainty as to the position which the coins bearing the names *Māḍharīputa* (C.CAI. Pl. XII, 4) and Vāsithīputa Srī Vadasata (id. 13. 14) should occupy in the Andhra series[2].

[1] BÜHLER, Ind. Ant. 1883, p. 272. The synchronism of Puḷumāyi and Caṣṭana is in every way probable and is rendered almost certain by the quotations from PTOLEMY VII, 1, 82 Βαίθανα (Paithan) βασίλειον [Σιρο]πτολεμαίου, and VII, 1, 63, Ὀζηνή (Ujjain) βασίλειον Τιαστανοῦ: BHAU DAJI, JBRA. VII, p. 117.

[2] BH. suggests that Māḍharīputa may perhaps be an Ābhīra (v. sup. § 84), and BHAND. (Hist. Dek. p. 35) that he may belong to a branch of the Andhra dynasty; but v. BÜHLER, Ind. Ant. 1883, p. 273; C.CAI. p. 107. For the coins of the Andhras: C.CAI. p. 102, Pl. XII; BH. JBRA. XIII, p. 3c3, Pll. III. IV; id. XV, p. 273, Pl. II; E.CSI. p. 28, Pl. II, 39—48; TH., Ind. Ant. 1877, p. 274; 1880, p. 61. Cp. also Proc. BA. 1882, p. 59; 1893, p. 117; JBRA. XII, p. 407; XIV, p. 153; PE. II, p. 66. For the chronology: BÜHLER, Ind. Ant. 1883, p. 272; BHAND. Tr. I. Or. Cong. 1874, p. 347; and Hist. Dek. p. 25 (rev. MISS DUFF, JRAS. 1895, p. 693); OLD., ZfN. 1881, p. 323 = Ind. Ant. 1881, p. 227.

§ 89. Nanda Kings of Kārwār. — Similar in style and fabric to the large coins of the Andhras, and, therefore, probably belonging to the same period, are those bearing the names of two Nanda kings of Kārwār.

C.CAI. p. 111; E.CSI. p. 31, Pl. II, 41. 42.

X. THE GUPTAS AND THEIR CONTEMPORARIES.

§ 90. The Imperial Guptas. — The founder of this dynasty, *Śrīgupta*, c. 260 A.D., and his son *Ghaṭotkaca*, are known only from the genealogical tables given in the inscrr. The coins begin in the reign of the third member of the dynasty, *Candragupta I* (**Plate IV**, 9), who is the first to use the imperial title *mahārājādhirāja*, and who is to be regarded as the founder of the Gupta era, the first year of which is 319—20 A.D. (SMITH, JBA. 1894, p. 165). The period of Gupta supremacy in Northern India begins with this date and ends with the death of *Skandagupta* c. 480 A.D. For this period the order of succession of the Gupta monarchs is certain, the limits of their reigns are approximately determined, and the series of coins is complete. After the death of Skandagupta, the attacks of the Hūṇas, which began during his reign (v. inf. § 103), and probably also internal dissensions led to divisions in the Empire. In the case of the divisions there remains at present considerable doubt both as regards the order of succession and the dates of the different reigns. This later Gupta period comes to an end in 606 A.D., when Harṣavardhana of Kanauj gained paramount power over the whole of Northern India (SMITH, JBA. 1894, p. 178).

The original capital of the Gupta empire seems to have been Pāṭaliputra (the modern Patna), and it is not improbable that the inscr. *Licchavayaḥ* which occurs on the *rev.* of Candragupta's gold coins together with the name of his queen Kumāradevī may denote that she belonged to a royal family of Licchavis previously reigning at Pāṭaliputra (BÜHLER, WZKM. V, 225 ff.; SMITH, JRAS. 1893, p. 81). When a great extension of the empire took place by the conquest of the kingdom of the Kṣatrapas of Surāṣṭra and Mālwa in the reign of *Candragupta II Vikramāditya*, c. 410 A. D., it is probable that the capital was transferred, either permanently or occasionally, to a more central position at Ayodhyā (SMITH, JRAS. 1893, p. 86). At its greatest extent the Gupta empire seems to have comprised the whole of Northern India, with the exception of the Panjab (SMITH, JBA. 1894, p. 178), which, no doubt, continued to be ruled by the Kuṣanas.

§ 91. The Imp. Gupta coinage. — The coinage of the main portion of the empire was originally of gold and copper. The types of the gold coins are borrowed at first from the eastern mintages of the Later Great Kuṣanas (v. sup. § 74, class (2)); but they show a development of their own and are, without question, by far the finest examples of Indian art. After the annexation of the kingdom of the Kṣatrapas, the Guptas continued in this region the issue of a dated silver coinage, exactly imitated from the coinage of their predecessors except that, in place of the caitya, a frequent Gupta emblem, the peacock, appears on the reverse. A silver coinage bearing this type, but of a somewhat different fabric, seems subsequently to have been struck also in other parts of the empire (v. inf.). The dates on the silver coins of Candragupta II Vikramāditya are not beyond dispute (FLEET, Ind. Ant. 1885, p. 66), but those of his successors, Kumāragupta I (121—136: SMITH, JRAS. 1889, p. 128, and JBA. 1894, p. 175) and Skandagupta (144—? 16*x*; **Plate IV, 10**: date, 145) are more certain.

The gold coins, at first, follow the weight-standard which the Kuṣanas seem to have borrowed from the Roman *aurei* (v. sup. § 70); but, later, there comes in another class of gold coins which seem to represent the Indian *suvarṇa* (= 146,4 grains or 9,48 grammes) and to be due to a revival of the ancient native weight-standard (v. sup. § 4). It is possible that coins of these two standards were in circulation together, and that they are distinguished on the inscrr. as *dīnāras* and *suvarṇas* respectively (FLEET, CII. III, p. 265; SMITH, JRAS. 1889, p. 43). During the reign of Skandagupta, the Roman standard is abandoned; but it is not equally certain whether or not the re-introduction of the *suvarṇa* took place at the same time or previously (RAPSON, NChr. 1891, p. 57; SMITH, JRAS. 1893, p. 105). The Gupta silver coins, like those of the Kṣatrapas from which they are imitated, seem to be intended for 'hemi-drachms' of the Persian standard (v. sup. § 8). It seems probable that this silver Gupta coinage, which was originally instituted in Surāṣṭra and Malwa in the reign of Candragupta II Vikramāditya, formed the pattern for a silver issue in the northern and central provinces of the empire during the two succeeding reigns. These silver issues — which may conveniently be called the western and the central — are distinguished by a difference in fabric, workmanship, and design: the latter are thinner and flatter, more carefully executed, and represent the peacock of the reverse with tail more fully expanded (SMITH, JRAS. 1889, pp. 121. 127; C.CMI. p. 17). A debased coinage of copper plated with silver bearing the names of Kumāragupta and Skandagupta, but having a trident instead of a peacock as *rev.* type, is probably to be attributed to Valabhī (v. inf. § 98) at a period when it was still a province of the Gupta empire (SMITH, JRAS. 1893, p. 137; cp. also BÜHLER, WZKM. V, p. 216). The copper coinage of the main portion of the empire shows a greater originality in its types, and appears to owe little to any preceding copper coinage (**Plate IV, 11**: Candragupta II Vikramāditya; SMITH, JRAS.

1889, p. 138, Pl. IV, 8—16; id. 1893, p. 133; JBA. 1894, p. 173; NChr. 1895, p. 167).

The three articles by V. A. SMITH, JRAS. 1889, p. 1; id. 1893, p. 77; and JBA. 1894, p. 164, form a digest of all work done in Gupta numismatics up to the dates of their publication. For full lists of authorities, v. JRAS. 1889, pp. 58. 59; id. 1893, p. 79, notes; JBA. 1894, p. 164 ff.

§ 92. Division of the Gupta Emp. — During the last quarter of the 5th cent. A.D., the western provinces become independent under the Senāpati Bhaṭārka of Valabhī (BURGESS, ASWI. 1874—75, "Kāṭhiāwāḍ and Kacch", p. 80; v. § 98); while the northern and central provinces (E.Malwa) were held by different branches of the imperial family; and, in other parts of the empire, powers previously subject or feudatory become independent. It will be necessary here to deal only with those to which coins can be attributed.

For a outline of the history of this period: FLEET, Preface to CII, III; SMITH and HOERNLE, Bhitarī Seal of Kumāragupta II, with Synchronistic Table of Guptas and Contemporary Dynasties, JBA. 1889, p. 84.

§ 93. Northern Guptas. — Three members of this branch in direct descent from Kumāragupta I Mahendra are known from the Bhitarī Seal. The name of the first is not at present certain. If read Sthira° (BÜHLER) it may, since Sthira is a synonym for Skanda, simply be another name of Skandagupta. If read Pura° (HOERNLE) or Puru° (C.) it must be the name of a brother of Skanda°. To this ruler have been conjecturally assigned the coins bearing the title Prakāśāditya (HOERNLE, JBA. 1889, p. 94; SMITH, JRAS. 1889, Pl. III, 9. 10; id. 1893, p. 125). His son, the Narasiṃhagupta of the seal, has been identified with the Nara(gupta) Bālāditya of the coins (HOERNLE, JBA. 1889, p. 93; SMITH, JRAS. 1889, Pl. III, 11; id. 1893, p. 128); and further with Bālāditya the conqueror of the Hūṇa Mihirakula (v. inf. § 107; HOERNLE, JBA. 1889, p. 93; C.CMI. p. 11. This identification has been doubted: SMITH, JRAS. 1889, p. 115). There appears to be no doubt as to the identification of Kumāragupta II of the seal with Kumāragupta Kramāditya of the coins (HOERNLE, JBA. 1889, p. 94; RAPSON, NChr. 1891, p. 50; SMITH, JRAS. 1889, Pl. II, 12; id. 1893, p. 129). All certain knowledge of the order of succession in this branch of the Gupta dynasty ends here; but it is possible that a Viṣṇugupta Candrāditya, whose coins bear a great resemblance to those of Nara(gupta) Bālāditya and Kumāragupta II Kramāditya, succeeded the last-mentioned (C.CMI. pp. 12. 19, Pl. II, 4). The last of this line was probably Śaśāṅka (**Plate IV, 15**), c. 600 A.D., the king of Kirṇa Suvarṇa, who seems also to have borne the name of Narendragupta (C.CMI. p. 12; SMITH, JBA. 1894, p. 172).

Coin bearing the name Śaśāṅka, C.CMI. p. 12, Pl. II, 5; SMITH, JRAS. 1893, p. 147. sCoins bearing the name Narendra, JBA. 1852, p. 402, Pl. XII, 11; SMITH, JRAS. 1893, p. 146; and JBA. 1894, p. 189. Kirṇa Suvarṇa = Rangamaṭṭī in the Murshīdabād Dist.: LAYARD, JBA. 1853, p. 281; BEVERIDGE, JBA. 1893, p. 315; SMITH, JBA. 1894, p. 172.

§ 94. Guptas of E.Mālwa. — This branch, which may perhaps descend in direct line through Skandagupta himself (C.CMI. p. 10), comes to an end, c. 510 A.D., or shortly after, when Mālwa was conquered by the Hūṇa Toramāṇa. Its last princes are *Budhagupta* (inscr. dated 165 = A.D. 484, and silver coins dated 174 = A.D. 493) and *Bhānugupta* (inscr. 191 = A.D. 510). The only coins known are silver hemidrachms of Budhagupta, and these, as might naturally be expected, are of the flat central Gupta fabric (§ 91).

SMITH, JRAS. 1889, pp. 8. 53. 134; C.ASR. IX, p. 25, Pl. V, 13; C.NChr. 1894, p. 252.

§ 95. Later Guptas of E.Magadha. — It is doubtful whether any known coins can be ascribed to this dynasty. The coins of much debased gold which were formerly thus attributed (SMITH, JRAS. 1889, p. 11) probably belong to the Northern Branch (v. sup. § 93).

For dynastic lists: C.CMI. p. 14; CII. III, p. 200; C.ASR. III, p. 137; id. XV, p. 166.

§ 96. Unattributed Gupta Coins. — No satisfactory attribution has hitherto been suggested for the following:—(1) gold coins bearing the name *Vīra(? sena or siṃha) Kramāditya*; date, probably 6th cent. A.D.; they weigh between 160 and 170 grains, or 10,36 and 11,01 grammes, and it is doubtful whether they should be referred to the Persian standard — didrachm = 172,9 grains, or 11,2 grammes, or to an Indian standard — 100 ratis = 182,5 grains or 11,82 grammes (SMITH, JRAS. 1889, p. 118, Pl. III, 12; id. 1893, p. 130); (2) gold coins of *Jaya(gupta)* (C.CMI. p. 19, Pl. II, 3); (3) silver coins, dated apparently 166 = A.D. 485, and having an inscr. containing *Śrī Harikānta* (SMITH, JBA. 1894, p. 195, Pl. VI, 15); (4) copper coins reading *(Śrī) Mahārājño (Ha)riguptasya* (C.CMI. p. 19, Pl. II, 6).

§ 97. Maukharis of W. Magadha. — These are known from inscrr. as the contemporaries and rivals of the Later Guptas of E. Magadha. Silver coins imitated from the central Gupta coinage, and bearing the names of two members of this dynasty are known — *Īśānavarman* (Plate IV, 13; a contemporary of Kumāragupta III of Magadha) dated 54, and 55 (SMITH, JBA. 1894, p. 193; C.CMI. Pl. II, 12; SMITH, JRAS. 1889, p. 136); and his son *Śarvavarman*, dated 58 (SMITH, JBA. 1894, p. 193).

There is some doubt as to the reading of these dates: FLEET, Ind. Ant. 1885, p. 68; and the era to which they should be referred is altogether doubtful, v. inf. § 105. Cp. also C.ASR. IX, p. 27, Pl. V, 20—22; and XVI, p. 79; CII. III, p. 200.

§ 98. Valabhī. — To the kings of Valabhī (Plate IV, 12) have been attributed certain silver coins bearing a trident on the *rev.* and inscrr. in debased characters which have not yet been thoroughly deciphered, but which seem to include the title *Bhaṭṭārakasa*. They are imitated from the western type of Gupta silver coins (§ 91). For earlier coins probably struck in Valabhī before the date of its independence, and while still tributary to the Guptas, v. sup. § 91.

C.ASR. IX, p. 28, Pl. V, 23. 24, reads the inscrr. as containing the names and titles of the founder of the dynasty Senāpati Bhaṭṭāraka (*recte* Bhaṭārka) and his eldest son Dharasena, but these readings are extremely doubtful. Cp. also C.CMI. p. 8, Pl. I, 16; HOERNLE, Proc. BA. 1890, p. 171, Pl. VII, 4a and b; TH. JBA. 1855, p. 509; id. JRAS. 1850, p. 63, Pl. II, 35—38; id. PE. II, p. 100; PRINSEP, JBA. IV, p. 687; NEWTON, JBRA. VII, p. 14; JBRA. VI, p. xxxix.

§ 99. Bhīmasena (Plate IV, 14). — In fabric and form of inscription these coins are, like those of Budhagupta, of central Gupta style (v. sup. § 94). They bear dates, which have not been certainly read, but which are presumably of the same era as those on the similar coins of Toramāṇa (§ 105).

C.ASR. IX, 26, Pl. V, 16; SMITH, JRAS. 1889, p. 135. For an inscr. of Bhīmasena: C.ASR. IX, p. 119, Pl. XXX.

§ 100. Kṛṣṇarāja (Plate IV, 17). — These coins of western Gupta fabric (§ 91) are found in the Nāsik Dist., Bombay, and have been attributed to a Rāṣṭrakūṭa king of this name, c. A.D. 375—400. This attribution is, however, certainly incorrect, as this date is too early for the style of the coins, which are imitated from the latest Gupta coins current in this locality. For the same reason it is impossible to place them so late as the time of the better known Kṛṣṇarāja Rāṣṭrakūṭa c. 756 A.D. Their attribution must therefore remain for the present undecided.

C.CMI. p. 8. Pl. I, 18. 19; C.ASR. IX, p. 30, Pl. V, 26; Fleet, Ind. Ant. 1885, p. 68; Bhāū Dājī, JBRA. XII, 214; Smith, JRAS. 1889, p. 138; E.CSI. p. 149.

§ 101. **The Nine Nāgas of Narwar.** — In the Purāṇas the Nāgas of Padmāvatī (= Narwar, C.JBA. 1865, p. 115; C.CMI. p. 21) and the Guptas of Magadha are coupled together, and the fact of their being contemporary is proved by the mention of Gaṇapati Nāga (**Plate V, 2**) among the tributary Rājas in the Allahabad Pillar Inscr. of Samudragupta (CII. III, p. 1 ff.). Names of six members of this dynasty occur in full on the coins, while portions only of two other names can be read.

C.CMI. p. 20, Pl. II, 13—25; C.ASR. II, 307; VI, 178.

Closely connected with these are certain coins having the inscr. *Acyu*, which must without doubt be attributed to the Acyuta mentioned in the Allahabad inscr. It is possible that this Acyuta may have been one of the Nāga princes.

Rapson, JRAS. 1897, p. 420; Smith, id. p. 643.

§ 102. ? **Parivrājaka Mahārājas.** — These tributaries of the Guptas are "said to have governed Ḍabhāla, perh. = Ḍahāla, and the country including the eighteen forest kingdoms" (CII. III, p. 93 ff.). It is possible that certain coins bearing the name *Rāṇa Hasti* may have been struck by the Mahārāja Hastin, whose inscrr. bear dates from 156 to 191 = A.D. 475—510. This attribution is, however, extremely doubtful.

CII. III, Pref. p. 8, and p. 95. For the coins: C.CMI. p. 8, Pl. I, 17; PE. I, p. 87, Pl. IV, 23 (coin found at Kanauj).

Closely connected in size and fabric with these are certain small coins on which the name Vigraha has been read (Rapson). Specimens were found by Ventura in the Manikyala Tope together with coins of the 7th and 8th centuries A.D.

PE. I, p. 94, Pl. V, 5—7.

§ 103. **Hūṇas.** — The Hūṇa invaders of India (called in Sk. lit. and inscrr. also Sita-, Sveta-, or Hāra-Hūṇas, v. Smith, JBA. 1894, p. 186) whose attacks, beginning during the reign of Skandagupta, c. 452—480 A.D., led to the dismemberment of the Gupta empire, were an offshoot from the Ephthalites or White Huns, a people of Tartar origin who settled in the Oxus territories, c. 420 A.D., and, from this date until the destruction of their power by the Turks in 556 A.D., waged almost incessant war[1] on the Sassanian monarchy.

The extension of this power to India followed the defeats inflicted on the Sassanians during the reigns of Yezdegerd II, 438—457, A.D., and Fīrūz, 457—484 A.D., in consequence of which the Sassanian provinces which bordered on India passed into the hands of the Ephthalites (C.NChr. 1894, p. 245). The leader of this invasion who conquered the kingdom of Gandhāra from the Kidāra Kuṣanas (v. sup. § 76) and established his capital at Śākala, probably c. 465—470 A.D., is known from Chinese sources as *Lae-lih* and has been conjecturally identified with the *Rāja Lakhana Udayāditya* of the coins[2].

[1] Drouin, Les Huns Ephthalites dans leurs rapports avec les rois perses sassanides, Muséon, 1895.

[2] C.NChr. 1894, pp. 247. 251. 279, Pl. IX, 12. The name read as *Lamata* by Th.PE. I, p. 411 (no. 4), and *Latona* or *Lanona* by Drouin, JA. 1893, (I), p. 548.

§ 104. **Hūṇa coinage.** — The most striking characteristic of the Hūṇa coins is their want of originality: they are, almost without exception, either adaptations or imitations of Sassanian, Kuṣana, or Gupta coins. They, therefore, afford valuable evidence of the progress and extent of the Hūṇa conquests. Those of the thin Sassanian fabric are, naturally, the earliest in date; and of these the class which bears inscrr. in the same modified form of the Greek alphabet as is found on the Scytho-Sassanian coins (v. sup. § 75) is no doubt older than the class which has Nāgarī inscrr., and may probably, in part at least, belong to the Ephthalites before their invasion of India (C.NChr. 1894, p. 262). Of these early Hūṇa coins, many specimens seem to be merely Sassanian pieces with the head of the Hūṇa leader restruck in *repoussé* (**Plate IV, 18**: Shāhi Javūvlaḥ) so that the reverse type — the Sassanian fire-altar — is almost obliterated. The species of coin thus produced was no doubt the pattern from which later coins struck in the ordinary manner were copied.

C. op. cit. p. 262; and cp. Pl IX, 10—15, with Il. X, 3. 4. These *repoussé* coins have been attributed to Kashmir, but this attribution depends on the identification of the Ṣahi Khingila (id. Pl. IX, 11) with Khinkhila Narendrāditya who is mentioned in the Rājataraṅgiṇī as a successor of Mihirakula (id. p. 265). This identification is however not certain, and the coins of Khingila would seem to be older than those of Mihirakula. The Ṣahi Jabūvlaḥ or Jabula of the *repoussé* coins is identified by C. with Toramāṇa (id. p. 253) on the evidence of the Kura inscr. of Mahārāja Toramāṇa Ṣāha Jaūvla; but this designation may be simply a tribal name applicable to any member of the dynasty v. BÜHLER, EI. I, p. 239; and SMITH, JBA. 1894, p. 189.

§ 105. Hūṇa coinage.—Other specimens are copies of the current Sassanian coins, and, in particular, of those issued during the latter part of the reign, i. e. 471—486 A.D., of Fīrūz (**Plate V, 3**). The first imitations, which most resemble their prototypes, have been found in great numbers in Mārwār, and have been assigned with much plausibility to the great Hūṇa conqueror, *Toramāṇa*, the son of Lae-lih, c. 490—515 A.D. (HOERNLE, Proc. BA. 1889, p. 228; JBA. 1890, p. 168, Pl. V). In any case they almost certainly testify to the Hūṇa conquest of the Lower Indus country and W.Rajputana. The Sassanian type thus introduced into India became predominant in the coinages of Gujarat, Rajputana, and in the Gangetic doab during, probably, the following three or four hundred years (v. inf. § 122). Evidence of the Hūṇa conquest of the later Gupta kingdom of E.Mālwa (v. sup. § 94) is afforded by the silver hemidrachms of Toramāṇa (**Plate IV, 16**), which are minutely imitated from those of Budhagupta except that the king's head on the *obv.* is turned in the opposite direction. These coins are dated 52, but the era to which this date refers has not been satisfactorily determined (SMITH, JRAS. 1889, p. 136; C.ASR. IX, Pl. V, 18. 19; C.CMI. p. 20, Pl. II, 11).

The following suggestions as to the era in which Toramāṇa's hemidrachms are dated have been made:—(1) FLEET, Ind. Ant. 1889, p. 228 supposes the date 52 to denote years of Toramāṇa's reign. This explanation is rendered less probable by the fact that the Maukharis Iśānavarman and Śarvavarman (v. sup. § 97) and also Bhīmasena (v. sup. § 99), apparently date in years of the same era (SMITH, JBA. 1894, p. 194); (2) DROUIN, JA. 1890 (XVI), p. 368, suggests a Hūṇa era beginning c. A.D. 448, and perhaps marking the date of the first invasion of India; (3) C.NChr. 1894, p. 252, supposes either that the date is Śaka with omitted hundreds, i. e. 52 =452; or (4) l. c. that it may refer to a Hūṇa era beginning c. 456 A.D. the date of the great victory over the Sassanians. For the dates of the known princes of the later Gupta dynasty of E.Malwa, v. sup. § 94.

§ 106. Hūṇa coinage. — The silver coins of ***Mihirakula*** (**Plate IV, 20**) c. 515—544 A.D., the son and successor of Toramāṇa, are of the Sassanian fabric only (C.NChr. 1894, pp. 256. 280, Pl. X, 3. 4; PE. I, p. 411). Copper coins of both Toramāṇa (**Plate IV, 19**) and Mihirakula (**Plate IV, 21**) are found which show at the same time the influence of both Sassanian and Gupta prototypes (C.NChr. 1894, pp. 265. 280, Pl. IX, 16. 17, and X, 1. 2; SMITH, JBA. 1894, pp. 195. 203). These are found chiefly in the Eastern Panjab and Rajputana, and, in some instances, the types and inscrr. of Mihirakula have been struck over those of Toramāṇa (FLEET, Ind. Ant. 1886, p. 245). This is the only class of copper coins which can be attributed to the Hūṇa Toramāṇa, but of Mihirakula other classes also are known. One of these bears the usual Kuṣana types (v. sup. § 74 (2); C.NChr. 1894, pp. 256. 281, Pl. X, 5. 6; SMITH, JBA. 1894, p. 203); while the types of another class (e. g. C. op. cit. Pl. X, 7) are of less certain derivation.

It is doubtful whether the copper coins of Mihirakula bearing Kuṣana types are not to be attributed solely to Kashmir, which the Kidāra Kuṣanas probably continued to hold after they were driven out of Gandhāra (v. sup. § 76) and which may, perhaps, have been conquered by the Hūṇas for the first time during the reign of Mihirakula. Against the suggested identification of the Hūṇa Toramāṇa with Toramāṇa of Kashmir: C.NChr. 1894, p. 256. For other Hūṇa coins doubtfully attributed to Kashmir, v. supra sub § 104.

§ 107. Hūṇa coinage.—Hūṇa coins of all types are found bearing names or fragments of names which are at present unknown from any other source. It is possible that there may have been more than one Hūṇa dynasty reigning at the same time; or these coins may have been struck by viceroys ruling over different provinces of the empire. The limit of date for Hūṇa coinage is probably 544 A.D., when, in the reign of Mihirakula, the Hūṇa power was broken up by a confederation of Hindu princes under Yaśodharman, Viṣṇuvardhana of Malwa, and Narasiṃhagupta Bālāditya of Magadha (C.NChr. 1894, p. 258). Fragments of this power may, however, have survived till a later date.

§ 108. Uncertain, Hūṇa or Persian. — There are some well-known classes of coins the nationality of which cannot at present be exactly determined. They show signs of their Sassanian orgin by their thin fabric and by the fire-altar which constantly appears as their *rev.* type. They have, therefore, characteristics which belong both to some of the Huṇa coins and also to the coins of the Persian kings of the Panjab and Sind. The best known of these doubtful series is that which bears the name of *Napki Malka.*

C.NChr. 1894, p. 267, Pl. XII, 2; Ar. Ant. Pl. XVII, 5, 7, 10, 17; DROUIN, Rev. Num. 1891, p. 221.

XI. LATER COINS OF N., E., C. AND W. INDIA.

§ 109. Persian Kings in the Panjab and Sind. — There are found in N.W. India coins of Sassanian type and fabric bearing inscrr. in Nāgarī, Sassanian Pahlavi, and an alphabet, hitherto unread, which is probably a development of the modified form of the Greek alphabet used by the Scytho-Sassanians (v. sup. § 75). These have been sometimes attributed to the later Hūṇas (C.NChr. 1894, pp. 267. 289), but apparently without sufficient reason. They were almost certainly struck by some Sassanian dynasty or dynasties — as is shown by the style of the coins and by the use of Sassanian Pahlavi — ruling over Sind and Multan, which the earliest Arab geographers include in the kingdom of Sind (Encyclopaedia Britannica, 9th ed., sub Multan). It may be noticed that this region had at other periods been in the hands of Persian conquerors (v. § 61, and cp. § 30). For one of these issues, which has the name *Śrī Vāsudeva* only in Nāgarī characters and all the remaining portion of its legends in Sassanian Pahlavi, an approximate date is fixed by its very near resemblance to a coinage issued by Khusru II Parviz in the 37th year of his reign = 627 A.D. (cp. LONGPÉRIER, Médailles des rois perses, Pl. XI, 3, with C.NChr. 1894, Pl. XII, 10 or Ar. Ant. Pl. XVII, 9). In the Pahlavi inscrr. on these coins Vāsudeva is called king of Bahman (= Bahmanvasi or Brahmanabad the capital of Sind), Multan, Tukān (= Panjab), Zabulistan, and Sapardalakṣān (perhaps = Rajputana; C.NChr. 1894, p. 292). The coins of *Shāhi Tigin*, which are closely connected with those of Vāsudeva and with the particular issue of Khusru II mentioned above, by the use of the same reverse-type, supposed to represent the sun-god of Multan (C.ASR. V, p. 123), also bear the title "King of India and Persia" (Nāgarī: *Hitivi ca Airān ca parameśvara*) = "King of the Panjab and Khorasan" (Sassanian Pahlavi: *Takān Khorasān Malkā*; C.NChr. 1894. p. 291). The attribution and interpretation of other coins belonging to this Indo-Persian class (e. g. C. op. cit. Pl. XII, 5—8) are less certain; but it seems probable that they belong to the same region and period as the others.

Cp. also WILSON, Ar. Ant. pp. 400. 402, Pl. XVII, 6. 8. 9, Pl. XXI, 22; TH., Hist. of Early Muh. Arabs in Persia, p. 90; PE. I. Pl. V, 10. 11; p. 122, Pl. VII, 6; II, p. 105.

§ 110. Kanauj (Kanyākubja). — Coins struck by princes of the following dynasties of the mediaeval kingdom of Kanauj are known:—

(1) *Raghuvaṃśi Dynasty*. For coins conjecturally attributed to Harṣadeva (c. 606—650 A.D.) v. inf. § 122. The silver coins bearing the inscr. *Śrīmad-Ādivarāha* were struck by Bhojadeva (**Plate V, 5**; c. 850—900 A.D.).

HULTZSCH, EI. I. p. 155; C.CMI. p. 49, Pl. VI, 20. 21. The same ref. also for other coins which may perhaps belong to this dynasty. For the mention in inscrr. of Śrīmad-Ādivarāha drammas and other contemporary coins, v. KIELHORN, EI. I, p. 169.

(2) *Tomara Dynasty*. The princes of this dynasty seem, at first, to have held both Kanauj and Dehli, and to have been confined to Dehli after the Rāṭhor conquest of Kanauj, c. 1050 A.D. The coins represent three consecutive rulers of both Kanauj and Dehli, c. 978—1049 A.D., and two others of Dehli only, c. 1049—1128 A.D. The gold coins follow the types of the Kalacuris of Ḍahāla (v. inf. § 116); the billon coins those of the Brāhman Ṣāhis of Gandhāra (Bull and Horseman type; v. inf. § 115 (6)).

C.CMI. p. 80, Pl. IX, 1—8; TH. PATHANS p. 58.

(3) *Rāṭhor* (*Gāḍahavāla*) *Dynasty*. The coins of the Rāṭhor conqueror of Kanauj, Candradeva, c. 1050 A.D., are not known. The series begins with those of his son *Madanapāla Deva*, c. 1080 A.D., and includes the coins of two other rulers reigning till c. 1193 A.D. The coin-types are like those of the Tomara Dynasty.

C.CMI. p. 82, Pl. IX, 15—17.

§ 111. The Pāla Dynasty of Magadha. — No coins of this dynasty are certainly known, but it is not improbable that the coins of Sassanian derivation bearing the name Śrī Vigraha should be attributed to *Vigrahapāla I* of Magadha, 910 A.D.

SMITH, JBA. 1894, p. 192; C.ASR. XI, pp. 175. 181, Pl. XLIII; C.CMI. p. 52, Pl. VI, 17. For the mention of *Vigrahapāla drammas* in the Siyadoni inscr. v. KIELHORN, EI. I, pp. 167. 169.

§ 112. Kashmir. — The origin of the Kashmirian coin-types is to be found in certain coins probably struck by Kaniṣka (v. sup. § 74, class (2)); and from this date until the Muhammadan conquest of Kashmir in the 13th cent. these coin-types — *obv.* King standing: *rev.* Goddess seated — remained unchanged. The workmanship, however, is so rude during the greater part of this period (e. g. **Plate IV, 24**: Jagadeva, c. A.D. 1198), that these designs were in some cases misinterpreted by the early numismatists; and the dead level of degradation is so constantly kept, that the evidence of date usually afforded by the progressive improvement or degeneration in style is here to a great extent lacking. From the reign of *Avantivarman* (c. 855 A.D.) onwards, the coins fairly represent the list of kings given in the Rājataraṅgiṇī. For all the previous period, the dates and order of succession given in the Rājataraṅgiṇī are untrustworthy, although a number of the names are found on the coins. That the Kidāra Kuṣanas held Kashmir for some time is certain, but the date of their settlement there is doubtful (v. sup. § 76). The Kashmirian coins of the Hūṇas given in C.NChr. 1894, Pl. X, 5—7, and 9—13 (v. sup. sub § 106), seem to be copied from coins of the Kidāra Kuṣanas; and those of the succeeding Nāga or Karkoṭaka Dynasty (c. 625—757 A.D., v. C.CMI, p. 39, Pl. III, 7—14) all bear the name Kidāra (Plate IV, 22: Yaśovarman). Between the date of the Hūṇa Mihirakula (c. 515 A.D.) and the beginning of the Nāga Dynasty, C. places a number of kings among whom a Toramāṇa occurs. This king has usually been identified with the Hūṇa Toramāṇa, the father of Mihirakula (RĀJENDRA LĀLA MITRA, Proc. BA. 1878, p. 191; FLEET, CII. III, Pref. p. 10 ff.). For the arguments against this identification and in favour of a somewhat later date for Toramāṇa of Kashmir, v. C.NChr. 1894, p. 256. Some gold coins of *Harṣa* of Kashmir (Plate IV, 23) c. 1090 A.D., are directly imitated from South Indian coins, for the attribution of which v. inf. § 125 (1).

C.CMI. p. 25, Pl. III—V; RODGERS, JBA. 1879, p. 277, Pll. XI. XII. Cp. also C.NChr. 1843 (VI), 1; PE. I, 388, Pl. XXXI, 1—15. For the reading *Tuñjīna* (STEIN) instead of *Turyamāṇa* (= Toramāṇa, C.CMI. p. 42, Pl. III, 1) v. SMITH, JBA. 1897, p. 6, Pl. I, 9.

§ 113. Nepal. — The earliest coins peculiar to Nepal are large copper pieces which bear some resemblance to the second class of Yaudheya coins — a resemblance no doubt due to a common origin from the coins of the Kuṣanas (v. sup. § 60). They appear to extend over a period from the first quarter of the 5th cent. to the last quarter of the 7th cent. A.D. Those bearing the name *Mānāṅka* have been attributed to Mānadevavarman, c. 425 A.D., and those reading *Guṇāṅka* to his successor Guṇakāmadevavarman, c. 450 A.D. These names occur only on the coins and in the native dynastic lists. No mention of them has yet been found in inscrr. or other dated records. The dates given are, therefore, only approximate. The coins of *Aṃśuvarman* (Plate V, 1) and *Jiṣṇugupta* can be dated with more exactness, as both these kings are known from dated inscrr. of the seventh cent. The coins bearing the names *Paśupati* and *Vaiśravaṇa* cannot be accurately dated. These are names of divinities, and it is uncertain by whom the coins were struck; but, from their style and fabric, they would seem to belong to the same period as the others.

C.CAI. p. 112, Pl. XIII; PE. I, p. 62, Pl. III, 12; JBA. 1865, p. 124, Pl. 15—19; BENDALL, ZDMG. 36, p. 651; SMITH, Proc. BA. 1887, p. 144, Pl. II; HOERNLE, id. 1888, p. 114. For the chronology: BÜHLER, Ind. Ant. 1884, p. 411; S. LÉVI, JA. 1894 (IV), p. 64, places Aṃśuvarman earlier.

§ 114. Ṣāhis of Gandhāra. — Traces of the kingdom which was established in Gandhāra — the Kabul valley and the region of the upper Indus — by the first Kuṣana conqueror (v. sup. § 65) are to found at intervals from its beginning to its end (c. B.C. 25 — A.D. 1026).

For a résumé of the information derived from literary sources, e. g. ALBERUNI, Hwen Thsang, and the Rājataraṅgiṇī, v. STEIN, Zur Gesch. der Śāhis von Kābul, 1893.

§ 115. Ṣāhi Coinage. — The coins may probably be arranged in the following periods:—(1) Coins of the early Kuṣanas, c. B.C. 25 — A.D. 180 (v. sup. §§ 65—73); (2) The later imitations of these (v. § 74), from which the coins of the Sassanian invaders (c. 300—450 A.D.) were copied (v. § 75); (3) The coins of the Kidāra Kuṣanas, who held Gandhāra, c. 425—475 A.D. (v. § 76). It is, however, doubtful whether these coins should be attributed to the kingdom of the Kidāra Kuṣanas in Gandhāra or in Kashmir; (4) The coins of the Hūṇas struck in Gandhāra, c. 475—530 A.D. (v. § 104). The use of the title Ṣāhi on Hūṇa coins is probably to be traced to this source; (5) After the Hūṇa period, during the visit of Hwen Thsang, c. 630 A.D., the king of Gandhāra was a Kṣatriya. This, perhaps, shows that the Kuṣana dynasty had become Hinduised (v. STEIN, op. cit. p. 5). It is uncertain what coins should be attributed to this period — perhaps the late imitations in copper of debased Kuṣana type (C.CMI. p. 49, Pl. VI, 1—6); (6) According to ALBERUNI (tr. SACHAU II, p. 13) a Brāhman vazir usurped the throne and founded a dynasty. To the different members of this Brāhman dynasty are attributed the series of coins commonly known, from their predominating types, as the "Bull and Horseman" coins (c. A.D. 860—950; C.CMI. p. 62; **Plate V, 6**: Spalapati); (7) For the remaining period which extends to the date of the suppression this dynasty by Mahmūd of Ghazni (i. e. c. 950—1026 A.D.), the names of the different princes are known from inscrr., but no coins have as yet been attributed to them. They are called Rajputs, and it has been conjectured (C.) that a counter-revolution may have wrested the kingdom from the Brahmans and restored it to its ancient Kṣatriya possessors.

C.CMI. p. 55, Pl. VII; Ar. Ant. p. 428, Pl. XIX, 1—23. For the supposed dates on the coins of the Brahman Ṣāhis v. BAYLEY, NChr. 1882, pp. 128. 291; TH., Ind. Ant. 1883, p. 260; FLEET, id. 1886, p. 185.

§ 116. Kalacuris of Ḍahāla. — Territory: the country watered by the upper Narbada and its tributaries (C.CMI. p. 67). Capital: Tripurī (= Tewar) for the ancient coins of which, v. sup. § 57. Of the mediaeval kingdom, the coins of only one monarch, *Gāṅgeyadeva* (**Plate V, 7**), c. 1005—1035 A.D., are known. On these coins, the ancient Indian type of the seated Goddess is retained on one side, while the whole surface of the other side is occupied by the inscr. They were imitated by the Candellas of Jejāhuti (§ 118), the Tomaras of Dehli, and the Rāṭhors of Kanauj (§ 110).

C.CMI. p. 67, Pl. VIII, 1—5; C.ASR. XVII, 71; ALBERUNI (trans. SACHAU) I, p. 202.

§ 117. Kalacuris of Mahākośala. — Territory: the present dist. of Chatisgarh and Raypur in the Central Provinces (C.CMI. p. 67). Coins of three princes, from c. 1060 to 1140 A.D., are known (**Plate V, 8**: Jājalladeva). As on the coins of the Kalacuris of Ḍahāla (§ 116), the inscr. occupies the whole of one side, but the type of the seated Goddess no longer appears on the other.

C.CMI. p. 67, Pl. VIII, 6—11; HOERNLE, Proc. BA. 1893, p. 93.

§ 118. Candellas of Jejāhuti or Mahoba. — Territory: the dist. bounded by the Jamna on the N., the sources of the Kiyān (or Ken) on the S., the Dasān on the W., and the Vindhya Mts. on the E. (C.CMI. p. 77). The coins represent seven of the nine known rulers between 1063 and 1282 A.D., and are copied from those of the Kalacuris of Ḍahāla (§ 116) to whom the Candellas were subject before A.D. 1063 (**Plate V, 9**: Hallakṣaṇavarma).

C.CMI. p. 76, Pl. VIII, 12—21; C.ASR. XXI, p. 77; HOERNLE, JBA. 1889, p. 34, Pl. IV, 11. 12.

§ 119. Cauhans of Dehli and Ajmir. — Conquerors of Dehli from the Tomaras (v. sup. § 110) c. ?1128 A.D., and of Jejāhuti (§ 118) in 1182 A.D. Those specimens of the Chauhan coinage which have been read with certainty represent the two last rulers, *Someśvara* and *Pṛthvīrāja*, from c. 1162 to 1192 A.D., the latter of these dates being that of the Muhammadan conquest of Dehli under Muhammad ibn Sam. The coin-types of the Chauhans are the Bull and Horseman (§ 115 (6)), which continued for some generations to find a place among the coin-types of their Muhammadan conquerors, the

Sultāns of Dehli (cp. S. LANE-POOLE, B. M. Cat. Indian Coins: Sultans of Dehli, Pll. I—III).

C.CMI. p. 83, Pl. IX, 9—14; BÜHLER, Proc. BA. 1893, p. 94; MORISON, WZKM. VII; TH., Pathans p. 63. For Rajput coins not certainly read, v. TH., Pathāns, p. 59; C.CMI. p. 88.

§ 120. Narwar. — For the coins of the Nāga dynasty, contemporary with the Guptas, v. sup. § 101. The later Rajput coins represent four of the six known princes between c. 1230 and 1290 A.D., including one — *Malayavarma Deva* — who is, at present, unknown from any other source. These coins bear dates in years of the Vikramāditya era (57 B.C.).

C.CMI. p. 89, Pl. X, 1—10; JBA. 1865, p. 115; TH., Pathans p. 67.

§ 121. Kangra. — The coins of the Rājas of Kangra represent a period probably from c. 1330 to c. 1610 A.D. They call for notice here merely as noteworthy instances of the survival of an Indian type — the "Bull and Horseman" — for many centuries after the Muhammadan conquest.

C.CMI. p. 99, Pl. XI; RODGERS, JBA. 1880, p. 10, Pl. II; BAYLEY, quoted in PE. I, p. 392.

§ 122. Unattributed Coins. — There are three classes of coins found in great numbers "from the Satlej eastward as far as Benares, and from the Himalaya southward to the Narbada River" (C.CMI. p. 47) which have not as yet been very definitely attributed:—

(1) thin pieces of silver derived from the Sassanian type. Those which are simply rude imitations of actual Sassanian coins have been assigned with much probability to the Hūṇas (§ 105). The later imitations, which show, as they recede farther from the prototype, a more degraded representation of the original types and an increasing thickness of fabric, are probably Indian; but they cannot at present be certainly attributed to any particular dynasties. They are "common in the Gangetic Doab, but are found more plentifully in Mewar and Marwar, and throughout all Rajputana" (C.CMI. p. 48). They may perhaps be the predecessors of the coins of class (2), or they may be independent of them though derived from the same prototype. In weight the two classes are similar; and, as the specimens vary from 60 to 65 grains, or from 3,8 to 4,2 grammes, they probably, like their Sassanian originals, represent the Greek drachma (v. sup. § 24). Some specimens bear the letters *Ha* or *Ja*, and C. (l. c.) has very plausibly suggested that the former may be the initial of *Harṣavardhana* of Kanauj. The later coins of *Bhojadeva* of Kanauj (Śrīmad-Ādivarāha) are, certainly, similar in fabric, and are probably derived from the same source (v. sup. § 110). He also suggests that those which bear the name *Śrī Vigraha* may possibly have been struck by some successor of Bhojadeva (CMI. p. 51); but it is, perhaps, more probable that they should be attributed to Vigrahapāla I of Magadha (v. sup. § 111).

C.CMI. p. 48, Pl. VI, 13—19.

(2) thick pieces of silver also derived from the Sassanian type, but so degraded in execution as to show little similarity to their originals. They are commonly called *Gadhiya paisa* (Plate V, 4) and C. (CMI. p. 50) would identify them with the *Ṣaḍboddhika drammas* of the Jaunpur inscr. (C.ASR. XI, p. 176). They are found in S.W.Rajputana, in Mewar, Malwa, and Gujarat (C.CMI. p. 47). By their *obv.* type they are connected with a class of coins, on which the name *Somaladeva* is substituted for the degraded fire-altar of the *rev.* The same name also occurs on coins which have for the *obv.* the "horseman" type, probably borrowed from the Brahman Ṣāhis of Gandhāra (§ 115 (6))

C.CMI. p. 49, Pl. VI, 10—12; BH.JBRA. XII, p. 325. Cp. also id. XI, p. 334; PE. I, p. 341, Pl. XXVII, 13—16.

(3) copper coins of very rude fabric which may perhaps be imitations of the coins of the Later Kuṣanas (class (1), v. sup. § 74) — *obv.* King standing: *rev.* Śiva and Bull. The workmanship is, however, so much degraded, that the *obv.* of these coins has usually been supposed to represent the Sassanian fire-altar. C. supposes these coins to have formed the common copper currency of the Panjab and Rajputana between A.D. 500 and 800 (v. sup. § 115 (5)).

C.CMI. p. 48, Pl. VI, 1—6.

XII. COINAGES OF SOUTHERN INDIA.

§ 123. General Remarks. — In the numismatic history of Northern India, landmarks of great importance are afforded by the successive foreign invasions. There are no such prominent landmarks to indicate the different periods in the history of the Southern coinages. At the same time the proportion of inscribed coins is smaller, and classification depends to a greater extent on arguments derived from the *provenance* of specimens, the nature of their fabric, and the style of their types. These coinages have, moreover, as yet not received a scientific treatment in any way to be compared with that which has obtained such valuable historical results from the coins of the North.

It is probable that the primitive method of punch-marking (v. sup. § 5) continued in use for a much longer period in the South than in the North; and, in some instances, it is clear that later improvements in the art of coin-making are the result of a development of this native method, and not of the adoption of the foreign method of striking from dies (v. inf. § 129; cp. also E. Numismatic Gleanings p. 12 = JMLS. XIX, p. 231).

Roman gold and silver coins (v. sup. § 14) are found in great numbers in Southern India and Ceylon, and it is probable that they were actually used as currency in these countries, while, in the North, the Roman gold coins may, perhaps, have provided some of the metal for the large gold issues of the Kuṣanas.

In the following list of South Indian states to which coins have been ascribed the Andhras are not included, as they have been discussed already, sup. § 85.

§ 124. Pāṇḍya. — Territory: the extreme south of the peninsula. After the punch-marked coinage, which here as elsewhere no doubt belongs to a very early period (v. sup. § 4) the most ancient Pāṇḍyan coins seem to be those, which, while retaining the original square form, bear a die-struck type — an elephant — on one side only; and, somewhat later, those which have types on both sides. It is almost certain that, in accordance with the usage of Southern India, historical facts are expressed by the heraldic symbols which occur on these coins in conjunction with the chief types, and it is, therefore, possible that the varying number of these symbols may afford data for a further chronological arrangement of the coins. These coins have been assigned to a period ending c. 300 A.D.; and the general resemblance which they bear in style and workmanship to coins of the Andhras (§ 87) and Pallavas (§ 128) makes this attribution not improbable.

LOVENTHAL, Coins of Tinnevelly (Madras 1888) p. 5, Pl. I, 7—15; TUFNELL, Hints to Coin-Collectors in S.India (Madras 1889) p. 8, Pl. I, 2.

There is much uncertainty as to the coins which should be ascribed to the Pāṇḍyas during the period c. 300—600 A.D.

For coins conjecturally assigned to this period: LOVENTHAL, op. cit. p. 7, Pl. I, 16—33.

Gold coins bearing the emblem universally adopted by the Pāṇḍyas in later times, viz. the fish, have been attributed to a period from the 7th to the 10th cent. A. D. (E.CSI. p. 120; **Plate V, 10**). Later copper coins show the influence of the Cola conquest in the middle of the 11th cent. A.D. (v. inf. § 126).

E.CSI. p. 119, Pl. III, 129—138; TRACY, JMLS. 1887–8, p. 138.

§ 125. Cera. — Territory: the province of Malabar. No coins have hitherto been assigned to the Cera dynasty at its most flourishing period before the Cola conquest in 877 A.D. After this date, certain districts over which the Cera power had been extended and which had hitherto been governed by viceroys became independent. Coins struck in two of such districts are known:—

(1) *Koṅgudeśa.* "The western part of Maisur as far as Nandidrug, together with Coimbatore and Salem" (E.CSI. p. 111). To this district have been assigned certain gold and copper coins on which the Cera emblem, a bow, is usually found together with other symbols. The date of these gold coins, the chief type of which is the elephant (**Plate V, 12**), is limited to a period before c. 1090 A.D., as they are imitated by Harṣadeva of Kashmir (v. sup. § 112). This coinage is apparently actually noticed in the Rājataraṅgiṇī, VII, 926 — *Dākṣiṇātyābhavad bhaṅgiḥ priyā tasya vilāsinaḥ, Karṇāṭanuguṇaṣ ṭaṅkas tatas tena pravarttitaḥ.* C.CMI. p. 35, translating Karṇāṭa as = Karnatic has accordingly changed the attribution of these coins; but Karṇāṭa seems to denote rather a district in the centre of the peninsula which included certainly a part if not the whole of Koṅgudeśa (L.IA. I, p. 170).

E.CSI. p. 111, Pl. III, 118—128.

(2) *Kerala.* This term, which is sometimes used as synonymous with Cera, is here used in its more restricted sense as denoting that portion of the Western Coast which lies between the Candragiri and C. Comorin (E.CSI. p. 61). To a dynasty ruling over this territory belongs a unique coin (TRACY coll.) in the British Museum with the inscr. Srī Vīrakeralasya in Nāgarī characters of, probably, the 11th or 12th century (**Plate V, 11**).

For the dynasty, the members of which bore this title, v. Sundaram Pillai, Some Early Sovereigns of Travancore, Ind. Ant. 1895, p. 249 ff.

§ 126. Cola. — The coins all belong to the period during which the Colas were becoming, or had become, the paramount power in S.India. They fall into two classes:—(1) before c. 1022 A.D. the beginning of the reign of Rājarāja Cola. These coins show that the Cola power was already becoming supreme: they bear the Cola emblem, the tiger, in the centre with the Pāṇḍya and Cera emblems (fish and bow) on either side of it. The coin-legends, in Sanskrit characters, give the names or titles of Cola sovereigns; but they have not, as yet, been identified beyond dispute with those occurring in the dynastic lists (**Plate V, 13**); (2) after c. 1022 A.D. With the reign of *Rājarāja* comes a coinage of an entirely new type — *obv.* King standing: *rev.* King seated (**Plate V, 14**). This type spread with the extension of Cola power over a great portion of Southern India. Its use was established in Ceylon, as a result of the Cola occupation of the island, and was continued by the independent Rājas of Kandy (v. inf. § 127).

E.CSI. p. 135, Pl. IV, 151—174; HULTZSCH, Ind. Ant. 1892, p. 323, Pl. I, 7; id. 1896, p. 317, Pl. I, 1. 2.

To a Cola sovereign, probably Kulottuṅga Cola I, A.D. 1070, have been attributed coins struck in *repoussé* on very thin gold, like those of the Eastern Calukyas, Calukyacandra and Rājarāja II (v. inf. § 130).

Hultzsch, Ind. Ant. 1896, p. 321, Pl. II, 26. 27.

§ 127. Ceylon. — The coins of the Rājas of Kandy, who adopted without any important modification the types of their Cola predecessors, represent a period from 1153 to 1296 A.D. (**Plate V, 15**: Parākramabāhu). Previous to this period the coins circulating in Ceylon have no distinctive character:—they are either of the ancient punch-marked pattern or are importations due to foreign commerce or invasion.

Rh. D., acc.; cp. also Vaux, NChr. 1854 (XVI), p. 121; PE. I, p. 419, Pl. XXXV; Lowsley, NChr. 1895, p. 211, Pl. VIII; Rangachari and Desikachari, Ind. Ant. 1895, p. 332.

§ 128. Pallava. — Territory: bordered by the Coromandel Coast. In the same region lived the Kurumbars, a people of considerable importance before the 7th cent. A.D. Between the coins of these two peoples no accurate discrimination has yet been made. The coins of this region fall into two classes:—(1) Those which in style bear some resemblance to the coins of the Andhras (e. g. E.CSI. Pl. II, 55—58, called Kurumbar; and perhaps also id. I, 31—38, called Pallava or Kurumbar), and may, therefore, possibly belong to the same period (2nd and 3rd centuries A.D.). The occurrence of the ship as a reverse type testifies to the foreign trade for which the Pallavas were famous. (2) The other class is of gold and silver and undoubtedly later; but here again there seems to be no evidence from which to determine the exact date. These coins all bear the Pallava emblem, the maned lion, together with Canarese or Sanskrit inscr. (**Plate V, 16**).

E.CSI. pp. 35 ff., Pl. I, 31—38; II, 49—58; id. JMLS. XIX, p. 237, figs. 48—50. 52.

§ 129. W. Calukya. — Territory: W. Deccan. After the beginning of the 7th cent. A.D. the Calukyas are divided into two main branches — the Western Calukyas in W. Deccan, and the Eastern Calukyas in that part of the Pallava country which lay between the Kistna and Godavari. The gold coins of both branches bear the Calukya emblem, a boar, and are remarkable as showing a particular application of the Indian method of punch-marking, by which each portion of a definite design is impressed on the coin by a separate punch.

Most of the coins of the Western Calukyas are of thick gold, and often cup-shaped (**Plate V, 17**). Elliot (CSI. p. 67) supposes these to have been imitated from the Kadamba *padma-ṭaṅkas* (v. inf. § 131) which are executed in the same manner and which he assigns to the 5th or 6th cent. A.D.; but there is no proof, in either case, of so early a date, and, on the analogy of the Eastern Calukya coins, they should probably be placed much later. For other coins attributed to the W. Calukyas, v. Hultzsch, Ind. Ant. 1897, p. 322, Pl. II, 28. 29.

E.CSI. p. 39, Pl. I, 19—23, Pl. III, 81—86.

§ 130. The dates of the known Eastern Calukya coins are fixed. Specimens in some alloy of bronze have been recently found near Yellamanchili in the Vizagapatam dist. bearing in the inscr. *Viṣama-siddhi*, the title of Viṣṇuvardhana, A.D. 663—672.

Madras Govt. Mus. Report 1894, p. 4; Hultzsch, Ind. Ant. 1896, p. 322, Pl. II, 34.

Other coins bear the name of Calukyacandra, or Śaktivarman (A.D. 1000—1012) and Rājarāja II (A.D. 1021—1062). On these coins the Calukya boar and each letter of the inscr. are stamped in *repoussé* on very thin gold. The attribution of these coins to the Eastern Calukyas seems to be beyond doubt;

but it is remarkable that most of the specimens known have been found in the island of Cheduba, off the coast of Arakan.

FLEET, Ind. Ant. 1890, p. 79; E.CSI. p. 67, Pl. III, 79. 80, assigned these coins to the Western Calukyas of the 6th or 7th cent. A.D. Cp. also PHAYRE, Proc. BA. 1872, p. 3. For specimens found in India, v. HULTZSCH, Ind. Ant. 1896, p. 321, Pl. II, 24. 25, who also points out that these coins bear dates in regnal years.

§ 131. Kadamba. — Territory: N.W.Deccan and N.Maisur. The gold Kadamba coins are in fabric and execution like the coins of the Western Calukyas (§ 129). ELLIOT assigns these *padma-ṭaṅkas* (Plate V, 18) — so called from the lotus which occupies the centre of the coin — to the flourishing period of Kadamba independence in the 5th and 6th cent. A.D.; but it seems probable that, like the coins of the Western Calukyas, they should be attributed to a considerably later period. The form of the Sanskrit letters which are found on them certainly supports this view.

E.CSI. p. 66, Pl. I, 7. 8. 10. 11. 13—17, Pl. II, 66—78,

§ 132. Rāṣṭrakūṭa. — Territory: the Kanarese districts of the Bombay Presidency. No coins have been attributed to this dynasty during its most flourishing period (c. 757—973 A.D.). For the silver coins, imitated from the coinage of the Kṣatrapas of Surāṣṭra, which have been attributed to Kṛṣṇarāja Rāṣṭrakūṭa, c. 375—400 A.D., v. sup. § 100.

§ 133. Kalacuris of Kalyāṇapura. — Coins of the second prince of this dynasty, Someśvara A.D. 1167—1175, are known.

E.CSI. p. 78, Pl. III, 87.

§ 134. Yādavas of Devagiri. — Territory: Kalyāṇapura and the northern districts of the Western Calukya kingdom (A.D. 1187—1311). For their coins, v. E.CSI. p. 72, Pl. III, 88—89.

§ 135. Yādavas of Dvārasamudra. — Territory: Maisur (A.D. 1047—1310). For their coins, v. E.CSI. p. 80, Pl. III, 90—92.

§ 136. The Kākatīyas of Worangal. — Territory: Haidarabad (A.D. 1110—1323); or their successors the Vema Reḍḍis of Kodāviḍu, A.D. 1361 — ? c. 1450 A.D. For coins attributed to these dynasties, v. E.CSI. pp. 82. 101, Pl. III, 93—95.

§ 137. Vijayanagara. — The rise of this kingdom is an important landmark in Indian history and numismatics; for while it became paramount in the country south of the Kistna and preserved there the S.Indian form of coinage, the country to the north of the Kistna had generally passed into the hands of the Muhammadans, and the Indian type of coinage had with a few isolated exceptions been superseded in that region by a coinage of the Muhammadan form.

HULTZSCH, Ind. Ant. 1891, p. 301, Pll. I. II; id. 1892, p. 321, Pl. I; id. 1896, p. 317, Pl. I, 3—6.

LIST OF ABBREVIATIONS.

Ar. Ant. = Ariana Antiqua.
AR. = Asiatic Researches.
ASWI. = Archaeological Survey of Western India.
BH. = BHAGVĀNLĀL INDRAJĪ.
BHAṆḌ. = BHAṆḌĀRKAR; Hist. Dek. = Early History of the Dekkan.
Bomb. Gaz. = Bombay Gazetteer.
B.M.Cat. = British Museum Catalogue.
C. = CUNNINGHAM; ASR. = Archaeological Survey Reports; CAI. = Coins of Ancient India; CMI. = Coins of Mediaeval India; Geog. = Ancient Geography of India.
CII. Corpus Inscriptionum Indicarum.
DR. = DROUIN; HE. = Mémoire sur les Huns Ephthalites.
E. = ELLIOT; CSI. = Coins of Southern India.
ed. = edited by.
EI. = Epigraphia Indica.
G. or GARD. = GARDNER; or GARDNER, British Museum Catalogue of Greek and Scythic Kings of India.
GUTSCH., Gesch. Irans = A. VON GUTSCHMID, Geschichte Irans.
Ind. Ant. = Indian Antiquary.
I.M.Cat. = Indian Museum Catalogue.
JA. = Journal Asiatique.
JBA. or JASB. = Journal of the Bengal Asiatic Society.
JBRA. or BBRAS. = Journal of the Bombay Branch of the Royal Asiatic Society.
JMLS. = Journal of the Madras Literary Society.
JRAS. = Journal of the Royal Asiatic Society.
JR. Geog. Soc. = Journal of the Royal Geographical Society.
L. = LASSEN; IA. = Indische Altertumskunde.
NChr. = Numismatic Chronicle.
obv. = *obverse.*
OLD. = OLDENBERG.
Proc. BA. or Proc. ASB. = Proceedings of the Royal Asiatic Society of Bengal.
PE. = PRINSEP's Essays ed. THOMAS.
rev. = reviewed by.
rev. = *reverse.*
RH.D. = RHYS DAVIDS; ACC. = Ancient Coins of Ceylon.
SBE. = Sacred Books of the East.
TH. = THOMAS; AIW. = Ancient Indian Weights.
Tr. I. Or. Congr. = Transactions of the International Congress of Orientalists.
WZKM. = Wiener Zeitschrift für die Kunde des Morgenlandes, or Vienna Oriental Journal.
ZDMG. = Zeitschrift der Deutschen Morgenländischen Gesellschaft.
ZfN. = Zeitschrift für Numismatik.

TABLE OF CONTENTS.

KEY TO PLATES OF COINS.

[When not otherwise stated, it may be assumed that inscriptions are in some variety of the Brāhmī alphabet.]

I.

PLATE I.

1. **Punch marked coin.** § 5.
Obv. A number of symbols.
Rev. Two symbols, one of which has been supposed to denote the district of Benares (C.CAI p. 56, Pl. I, 14).
AR. Wt 52,8 grains = 3,41 grammes.

2. **Guild-token.** § 6.
Obv. Steel-yard; Above, in Kharoṣṭhī characters, *Dujaka* or *Dojaka*.
Rev. In incuse, in Brāhmī characters, *negamā*.
Æ. [BÜHLER, Ind. Stud. III, p. 49 (sec. ed.)

3. **Persian siglos.** § 7.
Obv. Early Achaemenid king represented as archer half-kneeling to right. Punch-mark, symbol like *triskelis*.
AR. Wt 83,5 grs. = 5,41 grms. [RAPSON, JRAS. 1895, p. 876, Pl. 24.

4. id.
Rev. Incuse, and counter-mark resembling Brāhmī character *yo*.
AR. Wt 84,5 grs. = 5,47 grms. [RAPSON, JRAS. 1895, p. 875, Pl. 1.

5. **Persian double daric, struck in India.** § 7.
Obv. Achaemenid king (probably Darius III Codomannus, B.C. 337—330) represented as archer half-kneeling to right. Behind, :ΣΤΑ; beneath, ΜΝΑ; in front, ⚲.
Rev. Irregular incuse, with conventional pattern formed by curved line in relief.
AV. Wt 262,7 grs. = 17,02 grms. [HEAD, *Historia Numorum* p. 700. The inscr. behind and beneath the figure of the king on the *Obv.* has been supposed to mean "2 staters = 1 mina".

6. **Indian imitation of an Athenian coin.** § 9.
Obv. Head of Athena to right. Behind, [monogram]
Rev. Owl to right. In front, ΑΘΕ; behind, a bunch of grapes.
AR. Wt 257,8 grs. = 16,7 grms. [HEAD B.M.Cat., Attica p. 25, Athens, no. 267, Pl. VII, 3.

7. id.
Obv. Head of Athena to right. Behind, a punch of grapes.
Rev. Eagle to left, looking back.
AR. Wt 54 grs. = 3,49 grms. [HEAD, B.M.Cat., Attica, p. 26, Athens, no. 274, Pl. VII, 9.

8. **Sophytes.** § 9.
Obv. Helmeted head of king to right.
Rev. ΣΩΦΥΤΟΥ. Cock to right; above, on left, caduceus.
AR. Wt 58,3 grs. = 3,77 grms. [GARD. p. 2, Pl. I, 3.

9. **Diodotus.** § 12.
Obv. Diademed head of king to right.
Rev. ΒΑΣΙΛΕΩΣ ΔΙΟΔΟΤΟΥ. Zeus striding to left, hurling thunderbolt; aegis on left arm. At his feet, eagle to left; above eagle, wreath.
AR. Wt 257,1 grs. = 16,65 grms. [GARD. p. 3. Pl. I, 6.

10. **Demetrius.** § 18.
Obv. ΒΑΣΙΛΕΩΣ ΑΝΙΚΗΤΟΥ ΔΗΜΗΤΡΙΟΥ. Bust of king to right, wearing head-dress of elephant's scalp and diadem.
Rev. *Maharajasa aparajitasa Demetriyasa* in Kharoṣṭhī characters; Winged thunderbolt; below, right, monogram [monogram].
Æ. [C.NChr. 1869, p. 127, Pl. IV, 11 = GARD. p. 163, Pl. XXX, 3.

11. **Taxila; single-die coin.** § 56.
Obv. In incuse, left, pile of balls, right, *caitya*; beneath, wavy line and uncertain designs (? vine-branches).
Æ. [Cp. C.CAI. p. 61, Pl. II, 9.

12. **Pantaleon.** §§ 21. 56.
Obv. *Rājino Pamtalevasa*; Figure of Indian dancing-girl.
Rev. In incuse, ΒΑΣΙΛΕΩΣ ΠΑΝΤΑΛΕΟΝΤΟΣ. Maneless lion to right.
Æ. [GARD. p. 9, Pl. III, 9.

13. **Taxila; double-die coin.** § 56.
Obv. Elephant to right; above, *caitya*.
Rev. In incuse, maneless lion to left; above, *svastika*; in front, *caitya*.
Æ. [C.CAI. p. 62, Pl. III, 2.

14. **Maues.** § 29.
Obv. Head of elephant to right; bell suspended from neck.
Rev. ΒΑΣΙΛΕΩΣ ΜΑΥΟΥ. Caduceus; to left, monogram [monogram].
Æ. [Cp. GARD. p. 68, Pl. XVI, 1.

15. id.
Obv. ΒΑΣΙΛΕΩΣ ΒΑΣΙΛΕΩΝ ΜΕΓΑΛΟΥ ΜΑΥΟΥ. Poseidon, holding trident in left hand, with right foot placed on the shoulder of a river god.
Rev. *Rajatirajasa mahatasa Moasa* in Kharoṣṭhī characters; Female figure standing between two vines; below, right, monogram [monogram].
Æ. [Cp. GARD. p. 70, Pl. XVII, 1.

16. **Agathocles.** § 21.
Obv. *Hitajasame*, in Kharoṣṭhī characters; Tree in square railed enclosure.
Rev. *Akathukreyasa*, in Kharoṣṭhī characters. *Caitya* surmounted by star.
Æ. [BÜHLER, WZKM. VIII, p. 206.

17. **Vonones and Spalagadama.** § 30.
Obv. ΒΑΣΙΛΕΩΣ ΒΑΣΙΛΕΩΝ ΜΕΓΑΛΟΥ | ΟΝΩΝΟΥ. King on horseback holding lance to right.
Rev. *Spalahoraputrasa dhramiasa Spalagadamasa*, in Kharoṣṭhī characters. Zeus, facing, holding thunderbolt in right and long sceptre in left hand; below, left, monogram [monogram].
AR. Wt 36,5 grs. = 2,36 grms. [GARD. p. 99, Pl XXI, 10.

18. **Euthydemus.** §§ 18. 28.
Obv. Diademed head of king to right.
Rev. ΒΑΣΙΛΕΩΣ ΕΥΘΥΔΗΜΟΥ. Herakles seated to left on rock, holding in right hand a club which rests on rock; below, right, monogram [monogram].
AR. Wt 254,6 grs. = 16,49 grms. [GARD. p. 4, Pl. I, 11.

19. **Śaka imitation of coin of Euthydemus.** § 28.
Obv. Degraded imitation of head of Euthydemus.
Rev. Degraded imitation of type of Euthydemus; left, copy of name in Greek characters; right, inscription in Aramaean characters hitherto not certainly read.
AR. Wt 174 grs. = 11,27 grms. [C.NChr. 1889, p. 307, Pl. XIII, 5.

II.

PLATE II.

1. Miaus or Heraus. § 35.
Obv. Diademed bust of king to right.
Rev. ΤΥΙΑΝΝΟΥΝΤΟΣ Μ[or Η]ΙΑΟΥ | ΣΑΝΑΒ ΚΟΙΙΑΝΟΥ. King on horseback to right; behind, Victory with wreath.
AR. Wt 184,4 grs. = 11,94 grms. [C.NChr. 1888, p. 47, Pl. III, 2; GARD. p. 116, Pl. XXIV, 7.

2. Hyrcodes. § 36.
Obv. ΥΡΚΩΔΟΥ. Diademed bust of king to right.
Rev. ΜΑΚΑΡΟΥ ΑΡΔΗΘΡΟΥ. Armed figure facing, with flames issuing from shoulders, and holding spear in right hand.
AR. Wt 44 grs. = 2,85 grms. [C.NChr. 1889, p. 310, Pl. XIII, 15.

3. Zeionises. § 34.
Obv. Debased Greek legend probably intended to represent ΜΑΝΝΙΓΛΟΥ ΥΙΟΥ ΣΑΤΡΑΠΟΥ | ΖΕΙΩΝΙΣΟΥ; Satrap on horseback to right; various Kharoṣṭhī characters in field; in front, symbol.
Rev. Manigulasa chatrapasa putrasa chatrapasa Jihoniasa in Kharoṣṭhī characters; left, Satrap to right; right, City to left holding wreath and cornucopiae; Kharoṣṭhī characters in right and left field.
AR. Wt 149,6 grs. = 9,69 grms. [Cp. C.NChr. 1890, p. 168, Pl. XV, 1.

4. Strato II. § 33.
Obv. ΒΑϹΙΛΕΩϹ ϹΩΤΗΡΟϹ ϹΤΡΑΤΩΝΟϹ ΥΙΟΥ | ϹΤΡΑΤΩΝΟϹ; Diademed bust of king to right.
Rev. Kharoṣṭhī inscr. (for C's reading, v. GARD. l. c.); Athena to left, holding thunderbolt and aegis.
AR. Wt 37 grs. = 2,39 grms. [Cf. GARD. p. 168, Pl. XXXI, 7.

5. Rañjubula, imitated from coins of Strato II. § 33.
Obv. ΒΑϹΙΛΕΙ ΒΑϹΙΛΕΩϹ ϹΩΤΗΡΟϹ ΡΑΙΥ; Diademed bust of king to right.
Rev. Apratihatacakrasa chatrapasa | Rajubulasa in Kharoṣṭhī characters; Diademed bust of king to right.
AR. Wt 38 grs. = 2,46 grms. [GARD. p. 67; Pl. XV, 11.

6. Rañjubula — Rajubula. § 33.
Obv. Mahākhatapasa Rājubulasa in Brāhmī characters; Standing figure facing.
Æ. [BH. JRAS. 1894, p. 547, Pl. 4.

7. Hermaeus and Kujula Kadphises. § 65.
Obv. ΒΑΣΙΛΕΩΣ ΣΤΗΡΟΣΣΥ | ΕΡΜΑΙΟΥ; Diademed bust of king to right.
Rev. Kujulakasasa kuṣanayavugasa dhramaṭhidasa in Kharoṣṭhī characters; Herakles facing, holding club in right and lion's skin in left hand.
Æ. [GARD. p. 120, Pl. XXV, 1.

8. Kujula Kadphises. § 65.
Obv. ΚΟΡΣΝΑΚΟΖΟΥΛΟ | ΚΑΔΦΙΖΟΥ; Diademed head of king to right.
Æ. [GARD. p. 122, Pl. XXV, 4.

9. Kozola Kadaphes, imitated from Roman denarii of Augustus. § 66.
Obv. ΧΟΡΑΝϹΥ ΖΑΟΟΥ ΚΟΖΟΛΑ ΚΑΔΑΦΕϹ; Diademed head of king to right.
Æ. [Cp. GARD. p. 123, Pl. XXV, 5.

10. Nameless King, Soter Megas. § 67.
Obv. Diademed and radiate bust of king to right, holding in hand lance bound with fillet; behind, symbol.
Rev. ΒΑϹΙΛΕΥϹ ΒΑϹΙΛΕΥΩΝ ϹΩΤΗΡ ΜΕΓΑϹ; King on horseback to right.
Æ. [Cp. GARD. p. 114, Pl. XXIV, 2.

11. Hima Kadphises. § 71.
Obv. ΒΑϹΙΛΕΥϹ ΟΟΗΜΟ ΚΑΔΦΙϹΗϹ; Bust of king, wearing helmet and diadem, to left.
Rev. Maharajasa rajadirajasa sarvalogaīśvararasa mahiśvarasa hima-kapti(?)śasa, Śiva facing, holding trident in right hand, and antelope's skin on left arm; in right and left field, symbols.
N. Wt 123 grs. = 7,97 grms. [Cp. GARD. p. 125. Pl. XXV, 9.

12. Vāsudeva. §§ 72. 74.
Obv. ÞΑΟΝΑΝΟ ÞΑΟ ΒΑΖΟΔΗΟ ΚΟÞΑΝΟ; King standing to left; holding spear in left hand, and with right hand scattering grains on altar.
Rev. ΟΗÞΟ; Śiva facing, holding trident in left and noose in right hand; behind him, bull to left; above, right, symbol.
N. Wt 124,8 grs. = 8,08 grms. [Cp. GARD. p. 159; Pl. XXIX, 10.

13. Later Great Kuṣana. § 74.
Obv. The figure of the king is apparently imitated from that of Vasudeva, while the legend is a copy of that of Kaniṣka; Nāgarī characters — left, *ga*; middle, *gho*; right, *hu*.
Rev. Type of Vāsudeva.
N. Wt 120,2 grs. = 7,78 grms. [C.NChr. 1893, p. 120, Pl. VIII, 16.

14. Later Great Kuṣana. § 74.
Obv. Figure of king and legend copied from those of Kaniṣka; Nāgarī characters — left, *ha*; right, *vi*.
Rev. ΑΡΔΟΧÞΟ; Goddess seated on throne facing, holding noose in right and cornucopiae in left hand; above, left, symbol; below, left, Nāgarī character *la*.
N. Wt 121,4 grs. = 7,86 grms. [C.NChr. 1893, p. 119, Pl. VIII, 2.

15. Scytho-Sassanian: Varahrān V, 422—440 A.D. (C.). § 75.
Obv. Figure of king, copied from that of Vāsudeva, wearing head-dress ornamented with ram's horns; the inscr. in debased Gk. characters contains the name and titles of Varahrān.
Rev. Śiva and bull, copied from coins of Vāsudeva; inscrr. in debased Gk. characters.
N. Wt 121 grs. = 7,84 grms. [C.NChr. 1893, p. 182, Pl. XIII, 15.

16. Kidāra Kuṣana: Kṛtavīrya. § 76.
Obv. King standing to left; beneath right arm *Dharva*, and beneath left arm *Kidā(ra)*, in Nāgarī characters.
Rev. Śrī Kṛtavīrya in Nāgarī characters; Goddess seated.
N. Wt 120 grs. = 7,77 grms. [C.NChr. 1893, p. 201; Pl. XV, 11.

III.

PLATE III.

1. Kṣaharāta: Nahapāna. § 78.
Obv. Head of satrap to right; traces of inscr. in Gk. characters.
Rev. *Rājño Kṣaharātasa Nahapānasa* in Brāhmī characters; *Raño Chaharatasa Nahapanasa* in Kharoṣṭhī characters; Thunderbolt and arrow.
AR. Wt 29,2 grs. = 1,88 grms. [BH., JRAS. 1890, p. 642, Pl. 1.

2. Kṣatrapas of Surāṣṭra: Caṣṭana. § 80.
Obv. Head of satrap to right; traces of inscr. in Gk. characters.
Rev. *Rājño Mahākṣatrapasa Ghsamotikaputrasa Caṣṭanasa* in Brāhmī characters; *Cata(?)nasa* in Kharoṣṭhī characters; *Caitya*; right, star; left, crescent.
AR. Wt 25 grs. = 1,62 grms. [C.CMI. p. 6, Pl. I, 6.

3. Dāmasena, dated coin. § 83.
Obv. Head of satrap to right; behind, date 100+50+3, and traces of Gk inscr.
Rev. *Rajño Mahākṣatrapasa Rudrasīhasa putrasa Rājño Mahākṣatrapasa Dāmasenasa* in Brāhmī characters; *Caitya*; right, star; left, crescent.
AR. Wt 34 grs. = 2,2 grms. [Cp. Bh., JRAS. 1890, p. 653, Pl. 11.

4. Andhra: Gotamīputa, Viḷivāyakura. § 86.
Obv. Caitya within railing; above, *svastika*; right, tree.
Rev. *Raño Gotamīputasa Viḷivāyakurasa*; Bow and arrow.
P. [Cp. C.CAI. p. 109, Pl. XII, 6.

5. Siriyaña Gotamīputa Sātakaṇi. § 87.
Obv. *Siriyaña Sātakaṇisa Raño Gotamīputasa*, Head of king to right.
Rev. *Siriyaña Sātakaṇisa .... nasa Gotamīputasa*; right, *caitya*; left, "Ujjain" symbol (v. § 58).
AR. [E.CSI. p. 25. The *Rev.* inscr. differently read by BH., JBRA. XV, p. 305.

6. Vaṭasvaka. § 59.
Obv. *Vaṭasvaka* in Brāhmī characters; *Caitya*; beneath, pile of balls; right, standing figure worshipping.
Æ. [BÜHLER, Ind. Stud. III, p. 47 (sec. ed.).

7. Kāḍa: Cast coin. § 43.
Obv. and *Rev.* (similar) *Kāḍasa* in Brāhmī characters; above, snake.
Æ. [C.CAI. p. 62, Pl. II, 21.

8. Audumbara: Dharaghoṣa. § 43.
Obv. *Mahadevasa raña Dharaghoṣasa*¦*Odumbarisa*; across field, *Viśvamitra*, in Kharoṣṭhī characters; Standing figure of Śiva (or Viśvāmitra?).
Rev. Same inscr. in Brāhmī characters; right, tree within railing; left, trident battle-axe.
AR. Wt 37,5 grs. = 2,42 grms. [C.CAI. p. 67, Pl. IV, 1.

9. Kuṇinda: Amoghabhūti. § 50.
Obv. *Raña Kuṇiṃdasa Amoghabhūtisa Maharajasa* in Kharoṣṭhī characters; Deer to right facing female figure; above, symbol; below, *caitya*.
Rev. Same inscr. in Brāhmī characters; centre, *caitya* surmounted by trisul; right, tree within railing; left, *svastika* and another symbol.
AR. Wt 34 grs. = 2,2 grms. [C.CAI, p. 72, Pl. V, 1.

10. id. Chatreśvara(?).
Obv. *Bhāgavata Catreśvara Mahātmanaḥ* in Brāhmī characters; Śiva facing, holding trident battle-axe in right hand, and antelope's skin on left arm.
Rev. Deer facing left; above, symbols; right, tree within railing; left, *caitya* and symbol.
Æ. [C.CAI. p. 72; Pl. V, 5.

11. Kosambī: Bahasatimita. § 49.
Obv. Humped bull to right facing *caitya*; above "Ujjain" symbol.
Rev. *Bahasatimitasa* in Brāhmī characters; tree within railing; on either side, symbols.
Æ. [C.CAI. p. 74, Pl. V, 11.

12. id.: Cast coin.
Obv. Humped bull to left facing symbol.
Rev. Tree within railing; below, *caitya*; left, *dharma-cakra* and trisul; right, *svastika* and another symbol.
Æ. [C.CAI. p. 73. Pl. V, 7.

13. Yaudheya. § 60.
Obv. Elephant to right.
Rev. Inscr. in Brāhmī characters not fully read containing the word *Yaudheyana*; Humped bull to right, facing tree within railing.
Æ. [C.CAI. p. 77, Pl. VI, 2.

14. id.
Obv. Standing figure; symbol on either side.
Rev. *Yaudheyagaṇasya jaya dvi* in Brāhmī characters. Soldier standing holding spear in right hand.
Æ. [C.CAI. p. 77, Pl. VI, 7.

15. id. ? Brahmaṇya Deva.
Obv. Standing figure facing; right, tree within railing; left, trisul and *caitya*.
Rev. *Bhagavata Svamina Brahmaṇya* [*Deva*] *Yaudheya* .., in Brāhmī characters; Six-headed deity (Kārtikeya, *ṣaḍānana*, *brahmaṇya*) facing, holding spear in right hand.
AR. Wt 26 grs. = 1,68 grms. [C.CAI. p. 78, Pl. VI, 11.

16. Pañcāla (Śuṅga): Phalgunīmitra. § 53.
Obv. Figure standing on lotus; left, symbol.
Rev. *Phagunimitrasa* in Brāhmī characters; above, three symbols.
Æ. [Cp. C.CAI. p. 82, Pl. VII, 5.

17. Mathurā. § 52.
Obv. *Upātikyā* in Brāhmī characters; above, *svastika*.
Æ. [C.CAI. p. 86, Pl. VIII, 1.

18. Janapada. § 47.
Obv. Horse to left.
Rev. ...*putra Janapadasa* in Kharoṣṭhī characters; Tree within railing.
Æ. [Unpublished.

19. id.
Obv. Humped bull to left.
Rev. ... *Janapadasa*, in Brāhmī characters Standing figure.
Æ. [C.CAI. p. 89, Pl. VIII, 19.

20. Ārjunāyana. § 42.
Obv. Humped bull to left.
Rev. *Ārjunāyanāna* in Brāhmī characters; Standing figure; left, symbol.
Æ. [C.CAI. p. 90, Pl. VIII, 20.

IV.

PLATE IV.

1. Mathurā: Hindu prince, Rāmadatta. § 52.
Obv. Elephant facing &c.
Rev. In incuse, *Rājño Rāmadatasa* in Brāhmī characters; Standing figure; on either side, symbols.
Æ. [Cp. C.CAI. p. 88, Pl. VIII, 13.

2. Ayodhyā: Cast coin. § 44.
Obv. Fish to left; above, *svastika*.
Rev. Steel-yard; above, crescent.
Æ. [Cp. C.CAI. p. 91, Pl. IX, 3.

3. id.: Sūryamitra.
Obv. Peacock to right facing palm-tree.
Rev. In incuse *Suyyamitrasa* in Brāhmī characters; Humped bull to left, facing post.
Æ. [C.CAI. p. 93, Pl. IX, 14.

4. id.: Cast coin. Dhanadeva.
Obv. *Dhanadevasa* in Brāhmī characters: Humped bull to right facing symbol.
Æ. [Cp. C.CAI. p. 92, Pl. IX, 8.

5. Ujjain. § 58.
Rev. *Ujeni(ya)* in Brāhmī characters; above, man's hand.
Æ. [C.CAI. p. 98, Pl. X, 20.

6. id.
Obv. "Ujjain" symbol; below, river with fishes; left, tree within railing; above and right, other symbols.
Rev. "Ujjain" symbol.
Æ. [C.CAI. p. 98, Pl. X, 15.

7. Eraṇ — Erakina. § 46.
Obv. *Dhamapālasa* in very ancient Brāhmī characters written from right to left.
Æ. [Bühler, Ind. Stud. III, p. 44 f. (sec. ed.).

8. id.: Punch-marked coin.
Obv. Punch-marked with various symbols.
Æ. [C.CAI. p. 100, Pl. XI, 1.

9. Gupta: Candragupta I. § 90.
Obv. Right, *Candragupta*; left, *Kumāradevīśrīḥ*; Queen standing to right facing king standing to left.
Rev. *Licchavayaḥ*; Goddess facing, holding noose in right hand and cornucopiae in left arm, seated on lion to right; above, left, symbol.
AV. Wt 123,8 grs. = 8,02 grms. [Smith, JRAS. 1889, p. 63, Pl. I, 1.

10. id.: Skandagupta, silver, central fabric. § 91.
Obv. King's head to right, in front, date 100
40
5.
Rev. *Deva Skandagupto 'yaṃ vijitāvanir avanipatir jayati*, Fan-tailed peacock.
AR. Wt 34,3 grs. = 2,22 grms. [Cp. Smith, JRAS. 1889, p. 133, Pl. IV, 3.

11. id.: Candragupta II Vikramāditya. § 91.
Obv. King standing to left, with an attendant, right, holding an umbrella over him.
Rev. *Mahārāja Śrī Candraguptaḥ*; Garuḍa represented with human arms.
Æ. [Cp. Smith, JRAS. 1889, p. 138, Pl. IV, 9.

12. Valabhī. § 98.
Obv. King's head to right.
Rev. Inscr. not perfectly read; Trident.
AR. Wt 30,6 grs. = 1,98 grms. [Cp. C.CMI. p. 8, Pl. I, 16.

13. Maukhari: Īśānavarman. § 97.
Obv. Head of king to left; in front, date 54.
Rev. *Vijitāvanir avanipati Śrīīśānavarma deva jayati*; Fan-tailed peacock.
AR. Wt 35 grs. = 2,26 grms. [C.CMI. p. 20, Pl. II, 12; cp. Smith, JBA. 1894, p. 193.

14. Bhīmasena. § 99.
Obv. Head of king to left; in front, traces of date.
Rev. *Vijitāvanir avanipati Bhīmasena deva jayati*; Fan-tailed peacock.
AR. Wt 34,2 grs. = 2,21 grms. [Cp. Smith, JRAS. 1889, p. 135.

15. Śaśāṅka. § 93.
Obv. Right, *Śrī Śa(śāṅka)*; below, *jaya*; Śiva facing seated on bull to left.
Rev. *Śrī Śaśāṅka*; Goddess seated on lotus.
AV. Wt 145 grs. = 9,39 grms. [C.CMI. p. 19. Pl. II, 5.

16. Hūṇa: Toramāṇa, silver coin imitated from Gupta coinage. § 105.
Obv. Head of king to left; in front, date 52.
Rev. *Vijitāvanir avanipati Śrī Toramāṇa deva jayati*; Fan-tailed peacock.
AR. Wt 32,8 grs. = 2,12 grms. [Cp. C.CMI. p. 20, Pl. II, 11.

17. Kṛṣṇarāja. § 100.
Obv. Head of king to right.
Rev. (apparently). *Parama Maheśvaramahādevyoḥ pādānudhyāta Śrī Kṛṣṇarāja*; Humped bull crouching to right.
AR. Wt 31 grs. = 2 grms. [Cp. C.CMI. p. 8, Pl. I, 18.

18. Hūṇa: Shahi Javūvla, *repoussé* coin. § 104.
Obv. *Shāhi Javūvlaḥ*; Head of king to right.
AR. Wt 56 grs. = 3,62 grms. [C.NChr. 1894, p. 278, Pl. IX, 10.

19. id.: Tora(māṇa). § 106.
Obv. Bust of king to right; behind, *dha*; in front, *tra* (?).
Rev. *Tora*; above, wheel.
Æ. [Cp. C.NChr. 1894, Pl. IX, 16; and Smith, JBA. 1894, p. 200.

20. id.: Mihirakula. § 106.
Obv. *Jayatu Mihirakula*; Bust of king to right; in front, bull standard; behind, trident.
Rev. Fire altar and attendants, copied from Sassanian coinage.
AR. Wt 54,2 grs. = 3,51 grms. [Cp. C.NChr. 1894, p. 281, Pl. X, 3.

21. id. § 106.
Obv. *Śrī Mihirakula*; Bust of king to right.
Rev. *Jayatu Vṛṣa*; Humped bull to left.
Æ. [Cp. C.NChr. 1894, p. 280, Pl. X, 1.

22. Kashmir: Yaśovarman. § 112.
Obv. King standing; under left arm *Kidā(ra)*.
Rev. *Śrī Yaśovarma*; Goddess seated.
AV. Wt 112 grs. = 7,25 grms. [C.CMI. p. 44, Pl. III, 11.

23. id.: Harṣadeva, imitated from coinage of Koṅgudeśa (v. § 125). § 112.
Obv. Elephant to right.
Rev. *Śrī Harṣadeva*.
AV. Wt 71,8 grs. = 4,65 grms. [C.CMI. p. 36, Pl. V, 23.

24. id.: Jagadeva. § 112.
Obv. King standing.
Rev. Goddess seated; left, *Ja*; right, *ga*.
Æ. [Cp. C.CMI. p. 46, Pl. V, 32.

V.

PLATE V.

1. Nepal: Aṃśuvarman. § 113.
Obv. *Kāmadehī*; Cow to left.
Rev. *Śryaṃśuvarma*; Winged horse to left.
Æ. [Cp. C.CAI. p. 116, Pl. XIII, 4.

2. Nāgas of Padmāvatī: Gaṇapati Nāga. § 101.
Obv. Humped bull to left.
Rev. *Śrī Gaṇapatyu.*
Æ. [C.CMI. p. 24, Pl. II, 21.

3. Hūṇa: imitated from Sassanian coinage of latter part of reign of Fīrūz (471—486 A.D.). § 105.
Obv. Head of king to right.
Rev. Fire-altar; above, left, crescent; above, right, star.
AR. Wt 61 grs. = 3,95 grms. [C.CMI. Pl. VI, 13; and HOERNLE, JBA. 1890, p. 168.

4. Gadhiya paisa. § 122 (2).
Obv. Head of king to right.
Rev. Fire-altar.
AR. Wt 61 grs. = 3,95 grms. [Cp. C.CMI. p. 50, Pl. VI, 7.

5. Kanauj: Śrīmad Ādivarāha, Bhojadeva. § 110.
Obv. Viṣṇu in his boar avatar to right.
Rev. *Śrīmad Ādivarāha*; below, traces of fire-altar.
AR. Wt 62 grs. = 4,01 grms. [C.CMI. p. 54, Pl. VI, 20.

6. Ṣāhis of Gandhāra: Spalapatideva. § 115.
Obv. Horseman to right; behind, *gu*; in front, inscription in undeciphered characters (Tūrkī).
Rev. *Śrī Spalapati Deva*; Recumbent humped bull to left.
AR. Wt 50,6 grs. = 3,27 grms. [Cp. C.CMI. p. 63, Pl. VII, 6.

7. Kalacuris of Ḍahāla: Gāṅgeyadeva. § 116.
Obv. Four-armed goddess seated facing.
Rev. *Śrīmad Gāṅgeyadeva.*
AV. Wt 62 grs. = 4,01 grms. [C.CMI. p. 72, Pl. VIII, 1.

8. Kalacuris of Mahākośala: Jājalladeva. § 117.
Obv. Lion (?) rampant to right.
Rev. *Śrīmaj Jājalladeva.*
AV. Wt 57,5 grs. = 3,72 grms. [C.CMI. p. 76, Pl. VIII, 9.

9. Candellas of Jejāhuti or Mahoba: Hallakṣaṇavarman. § 118.
Obv. Four-armed goddess seated facing.
Rev. *Śrīmad Hallakṣaṇavarma Deva.*
AV. Wt 63 grs. = 4,08 grms. [C.CMI. p. 79, Pl. VIII, 14.

10. Pāṇḍya. § 124.
Obv. Two fishes under canopy; right, lamp; left, chauri.
Rev. Inscr. not certainly read.
AV. Wt 57 grs. = 3,69 grms. [E.CSI. p. 152 F; Pl. III, 129.

11. Kerala. § 125 (2).
Obv. Name not read.
Rev. *Śrī Vīrakeralasya.*
AR. Wt 36,3 grs. = 2,35 grms. [Unpublished.

12. Koṅgudeśa. § 125 (1).
Obv. Elephant to right.
Rev. Floral design.
AV. Wt 60,2 grs. = 3,9 grms. [Cp. E.CSI. p. 152 F; Pl. III, 119.

13. Cola. § 126.
Obv. Tiger seated under canopy to right, facing two fishes.
Rev. *Uttamacola.*
AR. Wt 62,6 grs. = 4,05 grms. [E.CSI. p. 152 G; Pl. III, 154.

14. id.: Rājarāja. § 126.
Obv. King standing.
Rev. *Rājarāja*; Goddess seated.
Æ. [Cp. E.CSI. p. 152 G; Pl. IV, 166.

15. Ceylon: Parākrambāhu. § 127.
Obv. King standing.
Rev. *Parākramabāhu*, Goddess seated.
Æ. [Cp. RH.D., ACC. p. 25, Pl. 5.

16. Pallava. § 128.
Obv. Vase on stand.
Rev. Lion to right.
AR. Wt 103,9 grs. = 6,73 grms. [E.CSI. p. 152 B; Pl. II, 49.

17. W.Calukya. § 129.
Obv. Boar to right, surrounded by various punch-marked symbols.
Rev. Striated.
AV. Wt 57,2 grs. = 3,7 grms. [E.CSI. p. 152, Pl. I, 19.

18. Kadamba: Padma-ṭaṅka. § 131.
Obv. Lotus, surrounded by various symbols and inscr. punch-marked.
AV. Wt 57 grs. = 3,69 grms. [Cp. E.CSI. p. 152, Pl. I, 8.

19. E.Calukya: Rājarāja. § 130.
Obv. Boar to right; *Śrī Rājarāja sa(mvat) 35.*
AV. Wt 66,8 grs. = 4,32 grms. [Cp. HULTZSCH, Ind. Ant. 1896, p. 321.

INDEX.

The references are to pages. Coin-legends are in *italics*. When one reference is of more importance than the others, it is placed first and separated from the rest by a semicolon instead of a comma.